Read On... Women's Fiction

Reading Lists for Every Taste

Rebecca Vnuk

Read On Series
Barry Trott, Series Editor

Libraries Unlimited
An Imprint of ABC-CLIO, LLC

A B C 🔆 C L I O

Santa Barbara, California • Denver, Colorado • Oxford, England

Library of Congress Cataloging-in-Publication Data

Vnuk, Rebecca.
   Read on— women's fiction : reading lists for every taste / Rebecca Vnuk.
       p. cm. — (Read on series)
   Includes bibliographical references and index.
   ISBN 978-1-59158-634-0 (acid-free paper)   1. American fiction—
21st century—Bibliography.   2. American fiction—20th century—
Bibliography.   3. Women—Fiction—Bibliography.   4. American
fiction—Women authors—Bibliography.   5. Women—Books and reading—
United States.   6. Fiction in libraries—United States.   7. Readers' advisory
services—United States.   8. Public libraries—United States—Book
lists.   I. Title.   II. Title: Women's fiction.
   Z1231.W85V58   2009
   [PS374.W6]
   016.3054'2—dc22   2009012315

13   12   11   10   09   1   2   3   4   5

This book is also available on the World Wide Web as an eBook.
Visit www.abc-clio.com for details.

ABC-CLIO, LLC
130 Cremona Drive, P.O. Box 1911
Santa Barbara, California 93116-1911

This book is printed on acid-free paper ∞
Manufactured in the United States of America

Contents

Series Foreword

Welcome to Libraries Unlimited's Read On series of genre guides for readers' advisors and for readers. The Read On series introduces readers and those who work with them to new ways of looking at books, genres, and reading interests.

Over the past decade, readers' advisory services have become vital in public libraries. A quick glance at the schedule of any library conference at the state or national level will reveal a wealth of programs on various aspects of connecting readers to books they will enjoy. Working with unfamiliar genres or types of reading can be a challenge, particularly for those new to the field. Equally, readers may find it a bit overwhelming to look for books outside their favorite authors and preferred reading interests. The titles in the Read On series offer you a new way to approach reading:

- they introduce you to a broad sampling of the materials available in a given genre;
- they offer you new directions to explore in a genre—through appeal features and unconventional topics;
- they help readers' advisors better understand and navigate genres with which they are less familiar;
- and they provide reading lists that you can use to create quick displays, include on your library web sites and in the library newsletter, or to hand out to readers.

The lists in the Read On series are arranged in sections based on appeal characteristics—story, character, setting, and language (as described in Joyce Saricks' *Reader's Advisory Services in the Public Library,* 3d ed., ALA Editions, 2005), with a fifth section on mood. These appeal characteristics are the hidden elements of a book that attract readers. Remember that a book can have multiple appeal factors; and sometimes readers are drawn to a particular book for several factors, while other times for only one. In the Read On lists, titles are placed according to their primary appeal characteristics, and then put into a list that reflects common reading interests. So if you are working with a reader who loves fantasy that features quests for magical objects you will be able to find a list of titles whose main appeal centers around this search. Each list indicates a title that is an especially good starting place for readers, an exemplar of that appeal characteristic.

Story is perhaps the most basic appeal characteristic. It relates to the plot of the book—what are the elements of the tale? Is the emphasis more on the people or the situations? Is the story action focused or more interior? Is it funny? Scary?

Many readers are drawn to the books they love by the characters. The character appeal reflects such aspects as whether there are lots of characters or only a single main character; are the characters easily recognizable types? Do the characters grow and change over the course of the story? What are the characters' occupations?

Setting covers a range of elements that might appeal to readers. What is the time period or geographic locale of the tale? How much does the author describe the surroundings of the story? Does the reader feel as though he or she is "there" when reading the book? Are there special features such as the monastic location of Ellis Peters' Brother Cadfael mysteries or the small town setting of Jan Karon's Mitford series?

Although not traditionally considered an appeal characteristic, mood is important to readers as well. It relates to how the author uses the tools of narrative—language, pacing, story, and character—to create a feeling for the work. Mood can be difficult to quantify because the reader brings his or her own feelings to the story as well. Mood really asks how does the book make the reader feel? Creepy? Refreshed? Joyful? Sad?

Finally, the language appeal brings together titles where the author's writing style draws the reader. This can be anything from a lyrical prose style with lots of flourishes to a spare use of language à la Hemingway. Humor, snappy dialog, wordplay, recipes and other language elements all have the potential to attract readers.

Dig into these lists. Use them to find new titles and authors in a genre that you love, or as a guide to expand your knowledge of a new type of writing. Above all, read, enjoy, and remember—never apologize for your reading tastes!

Barry Trott
Series Editor

Acknowledgments

I would like to thank the wonderful reader's advisory librarians I have had the pleasure to know—most especially the dedicated members of the Adult Reading Round Table in Illinois. Special thanks to Eugenia Bryant and Merle Jacob for their mentoring, friendship, and for giving me opportunities to practice the craft. Eugenia, I cut my annotating teeth on MatchBook, so this one's for you! Thanks to Libraries Unlimited editor Barbara Ittner, for giving me many good names of lists to start the creative juices flowing, thanks to series editor Barry Trott for his guidance and patience, and thank you to Mom, Dad, Ken, and Kenny.

Introduction

Women's Fiction Defined

Is women's fiction a genre? If so, it is probably the least "genre-y" of genres. Why do I say that? Mainly because the stories can follow any number of directions—they can be romantic, they can be suspenseful, they can be funny, they can be sad, but the thread holding them together is that the central character or characters are women. And the main thrust of the story is the life of women, rather than suspense, for example. In any case, for the purpose of continuity, this guide will refer to the books as a genre.

These are novels exploring the lives of female protagonists, with a focus on their relationships with family, friends, and lovers. Some books are characterized by a romantic tone; there may be elements of adventure or mystery as well, but the main theme is of a woman overcoming and learning from crises, and emerging triumphant. One current trend is to employ a lighter, sometimes even tongue-in-cheek tone. But overall, emotions and relationships are the common thread between books that can be classified in this genre.

Harper Collins/Avon senior editor Micki Nuding explains, "Women's Fiction can be commercial (and usually is) or literary; it can be here-and-now contemporary or a multigenerational saga. The woman is the star of the story and her changes and emotional development are the subject."[1]

So how do you know if a book is a romance or "just" women's fiction? After all, the characters do fall in love in a large percentage of women's fiction novels, and boyfriends, husbands, and lovers show up as main characters as well.

For starters, a man (or a hero) might be waiting for the heroine of these novels at the end of her journey, but he does not usually get equal time or equal depth to his internal journey during the course of a book. In romances, the author renders the hero in every detail—fulfilling an expectation of readers. Another expectation in romance is the "happily ever after" ending—which does not matter in women's fiction.

Literary fiction is another category that can be argued over. Can women's fiction be serious, can it have lush language, or does that move it over to literary fiction? Again, I think this is one of the thorny issues with defining these genres, as every reader has a different reaction to the appeal characteristics. There is plenty of literary fiction that has heart and soul to the story, but just because a novel is written by a woman and has female protagonists, it doesn't mean it has the same style and appeal that would make it women's fiction.

Further muddying the waters, a book can certainly be classified in more than one genre. Paranormal romance and historical fantasy are good examples of this issue. There are also many historical novels that really deal with women's fiction issues just as much as the details of the time period in which they are set. As you can see, women fiction is very hard to define.

Appeal

Is it too cheeky to say that the main audience for women's fiction is... women? While there are certainly men who enjoy a good story no matter what the gender of the characters, it's safe to say that these books are written for women readers. Women like the reality of the stories, the characters who are easy to identify with, and the exploration of emotions.

The two main categories of appeal for this genre are characters and storyline, which tend to be intertwined. Often times, readers enjoy women's fiction because they can identify with a character (or sometimes, it's a feeling of relief that they are not like a particular character!). A large part of the appeal of these books is one of recognition—feeling as though you are that character, you know that character, or you recognize what that character is going through. As a devoted reader of the genre, I can attest that when I read women's fiction, I want to see myself or the people I know on the pages of these books; and if not that, then a character leading a life I'd like to have! Because the storyline of the books focuses on relationships, characters are important. Pacing is not a defining feature of this genre, as it varies widely from book to book—some novels are slow and you can sink your teeth into them, others are quick and frothy reads. Language is also not a huge part of the genre's appeal, because women's fiction can be chatty, it can be introspective, it can be literary—there is not one single characteristic of language that defines the genre.

An interesting point to note is that while this genre is generally made up of contemporary books, about present-day issues (making it a very fluid genre), there are also books set in past time periods that showcase universal themes still relevant for today's women.

History and Trends

We've come a long way, baby, since the days when women wrote under a male pen name or using their initials in order to get their work published. Early feminist writers and 19th-century writers of domestic fiction can be credited with the creation of this genre. Louisa May Alcott (*Moods,* 1864), Jane Austen (*Pride and Prejudice,* 1813), Willa Cather (*Lucy Gayheart,* 1935), and Rebecca West (*Harriet Hume,* 1929) wrote about the women of their times and what they were going through as far as family and relationships were concerned. Authors from the 1950s through the 1990s, not represented in the following lists, include Erica Jong (*Any Woman's Blues,* 1990), Mary McCarthy (*A Charmed Life,* 1955), Elizabeth Cadell (*My Dear Aunt Flora,* 1946), and Helen Van Slyke (*Sisters and Strangers,* 1978).

There are two subgroups of women's fiction that have gained popularity in the last decade. Chick lit, kicked off in the late 1990s with *Bridget Jones's Diary* by Helen Fielding, is a sub-genre with titles focusing on single, 20- or 30-something protagonists usually trying to find their way in life, in the big city or in a new fabulous career. These books are humorous and generally lighthearted. (And if there are shoes or legs on the cover, you know that's what you're reading.) On the flip side, issue-driven titles are darker, dealing with family problems and issues—more hot topic, Oprah-esque tales. Issue-driven novels continue to increase in popularity, even without the assistance of Oprah's book club.

There has been a lot of talk regarding the demise of chick lit, but someone forgot to tell the publishers who keep putting them out and the readers who keep reading and enjoying them. There has been plenty of criticism of chick lit as well. After all, once chick lit became hot, authors scrambled to write their frothy, fun commercial successes at breakneck speed, publishers rushed to put them out, and before long, the market was saturated with books that looked and sounded alike, far too many for the consumer to read or even process. And so, perhaps the trend is coming to an end. However, there has been quite a bit of branching out from the single-in-the-city books, with mommy lit dominating the publishing houses recently. And there has been a smooth blurring of the edges—it's often harder these days to pigeon hole something as chick lit instead of simply women's fiction.

Ensemble fiction, featuring a number of characters brought together by a common interest, is gaining new ground. From novels featuring craft circles, to book clubs, to reuniting college friends, ensemble fiction is taking the genre by storm. Again, this speaks to the appeal of women wanting to read about characters that are like themselves, or who they would like to be.

How to Use This Book

This book is intended for anyone who loves women's fiction—librarians, reader's advisors, book club leaders, and the general reader. The lists are not intended to be comprehensive, nor exclusive, but rather a good place to find books of similar theme or appeal for when a reader is hungry for something in the same vein of a book they just enjoyed.

The lists are sorted alphabetically by author, with an arrow indicating the best of the list. While the definition of a "good book" naturally varies from reader to reader, the titles accompanied by an arrow are of standout quality for the noted appeal characteristic, and generally popular with readers.

Some readers may note that certain books cut across several themes and appeal characteristics. I attempted to choose the main characteristic of the story when assigning a book to a list. The annotations are intended to give you a good idea of what the story is about, and why it is appealing. The edition information given is usually for the first edition, with reprints noted.

Purists will note that early writers, such as Jane Austen, do not appear throughout, but they are featured in their own list in the language section (Classics in the Field). This is not meant to demean the beginnings of the genre. Entire college courses are devoted to women writers, but this book may not be likely to have a place on the syllabus. The focus of this book is strictly *contemporary* women's fiction. An effort was made to keep romance fiction off of the lists, as well, because that's a whole separate book in itself. Of course, some crossover could not be avoided, however, as many romance novels describe a woman's full relationships, not just her romantic relationships. For example, as much as I know Nora Roberts and Susan Elizabeth Phillips consider themselves romance writers, I felt remiss leaving them out of the game, since so many readers don't really care what the classification of a book is, they care about what makes it a good read. It was also a challenge to keep books with a historical setting out of the lists, but I felt that often times, historical fiction focuses more on the time period than the relationships of the characters. Again, there will always be exceptions, and books that feature the women as much as the setting have been listed to showcase the breadth and range of women's fiction.

Truly, there are a great number of authors that may or may not belong on these lists, and I had to make the call. Jan Karon is another good example, but my feeling was that her books are more inspirational fiction, and, her main character is male. And Barbara Kingsolver does not appear, because her books have a variety of characters and are not limited to women's issues.

In general, I hope these lists inspire readers to try a new author, to find something they may not have read before, and to thoroughly enjoy getting lost in a good book.

Note

1. Lisa Craig, "Women's Fiction vs. Romance: A Tale of Two Genres," *Writing-World.com,* http://www.writing-world.com/romance/craig.shtml.

Chapter One

Story

Story is the most basic appeal characteristic, and it's definitely one of the strongest features of the women's fiction genre. Readers know that when they start a book in this genre, they will be treated to a good story—likely featuring characters they can relate to, a plot that they recognize, and just enough depth for them to sink their teeth into, without making them work too hard to get something out of it.

The books in these lists are varied in theme, from stories of women wronged to stories of women who get a second chance in life. Some are fun, some are dramatic, but they all have interesting plots no matter what the subject at hand. Overwhelmingly, the storylines in this genre are contemporary. Readers are looking for current issues and topics.

James Baldwin perhaps said it best: "You think your pain and your heart-break are unprecedented in the history of the world, but then you read."[1] These novels connect readers to the emotions and predicaments of other women through their stories, whether familiar or fantasy.

Oh No He Didn't!

Stories of women wronged—not revenge stories as such, but more women triumphing over being jilted.

Andrews, Mary Kay
⇨ *Hissy Fit.* 2004. HarperCollins. ISBN 0060564644. 432p.

Keeley Ray, an interior designer in small-town Georgia, catches her fiancé and the maid of honor getting it on the day before the wedding. After throwing a hissy fit (and a good one!) she finds herself and her business ostracized. When a wealthy businessman hires her to redo his historical home, she can't help but fall for him, and the two of them hatch a plan to catapult her back into business.

Buchan, Elizabeth

Revenge of the Middle-Aged Woman. 2003. Viking. ISBN 0670032069. 368p.

London editor Rose is devastated when her husband of 25 years leaves her. What makes matters worse is that his new girlfriend is Rose's former assistant, Minty, who has also managed to steal Rose's job. As she picks up the pieces of her shattered life, Rose realizes that living well is the best revenge. Followed by Minty's story in *Wives Behaving Badly* (2006).

Green, Jane

To Have and to Hold. 2004. Broadway. ISBN 0767912268. 432p.

Plain-Jane Alice has let herself be molded into a perfect wife by her cheating boor of a husband. When he gets caught philandering in a boardroom, his London firm sends him to the United States. She hopes it will be a new beginning for them—but it really turns into a new beginning for her. Alice starts to rediscover her old self and extricate herself from the man who doesn't deserve her.

Kaplan, Janice, and Lynn Schnurnberger

The Men I Didn't Marry. 2006. Ballantine. ISBN 0345490703. 304p.

Hallie is a successful lawyer and mother looking forward to reconnecting with her husband as her college-age kids move out. She's devastated when her husband of 21 years tells her that he is leaving her for his 20-year-old fitness instructor. After a bit of wallowing, she decides perhaps her new future can be found in her past, and seeks out all of her old boyfriends, with comic results.

Keyes, Marian

Watermelon. 1995. Avon. ISBN 038097617X. 417p.

Claire is shocked, to say the least, when her seemingly perfect husband walks out on her the day she gives birth to their first child. She takes refuge in her quirky but loving family back in Dublin and figures out how to reconstruct her life, new baby in tow. When her hubby comes back contrite, what will Claire do? A laugh-out-loud read of a woman triumphing over what could possibly be the worst betrayal by a husband ever.

Lipman, Elinor

Isabel's Bed. 1995. Pocket. ISBN 0671881604. 387p.

Harriet is unceremoniously kicked out by her boyfriend of over a decade—so he can marry his new, younger girlfriend. Homeless and unsure of her path in life, she retreats to Cape Cod to ghostwrite the autobiography of a woman who was involved in a scandalous murder case. The two women become friends, and Harriet learns more about herself and who she wants to be.

Lutz, Karen McCullah
The Bachelorette Party. 2005. St. Martin's. ISBN 031232619X. 248p.

Still reeling after being literally left at the altar, Zadie has sworn off love and can't understand why her best friend, Gray, would want to marry her uptight cousin Helen. When Helen goes wild at her bachelorette party, Zadie has to decide whether she should tattle about the bride-to-be's bad behavior. Is she just jealous and still hurt from being dumped, or is she looking out for her friend?

Getting Crafty

From knitting to quilting, these books mix friendship with crafts, just like many women do in real life!

Battle, Lois
The Florabama Ladies' Auxiliary & Sewing Circle. 2001. Viking. ISBN 0670894699. 358p.

Bonnie, used to the silver spoon life, strikes out on her own after she divorces her bankrupt husband. She settles in the small town of Florabama, Alabama, where she takes a job coordinating an education program for women who have lost their sewing factory jobs. She encourages the women to start a sewing group and they all begin to realize their worth and independence, including Bonnie.

Chiaverini, Jennifer
⇨ *The Quilter's Apprentice.* **Elm Creek Quilts Series.** 1999. Simon & Schuster. ISBN0684849720. 272p.

In the first book of 11 set in a small Pennsylvania college town, Chiaverini introduces readers to Sarah, new in town and bored. A former accountant, she decides she needs a radical change and takes a job housekeeping for an elderly matriarch and master quilter, Sylvia, on the condition that Sylvia will teach her to knit. Chiaverini's quilt-themed novels are so popular, they have even spawned a signature line of fabrics.

Dallas, Sandra
Persian Pickle Club. 1995. St. Martin's. ISBN 0312135866. 196p.

Set in Depression-era Kansas, this is the story of Rita and the quilting circle she joins with an ulterior motive—an aspiring journalist, she wants to investigate the mysterious death of one of the club ladies' husbands. The women band together to keep long-held secrets.

Hood, Ann
The Knitting Circle. 2007. W.W. Norton. ISBN 9780393059014. 384p.

Mary loses her young daughter to a sudden illness. To cope with her grief and distract her mind, she joins a knitting circle. The people she meets there help her to come to terms with her tragedy—as she goes through the stages of mourning, she learns a new stitch from each person, and also learns something about their past.

Jacobs, Kathleen
The Friday Night Knitting Club. 2006. Putnam. ISBN 9780399154096. 352p.

Georgia runs a Manhattan yarn shop, Walker and Daughter. After she begins a Friday night knitting club, she becomes friends with the diverse group of women who join up. There's handbag designer Peri, TV producer and first-time single mom Lucie, and feminist grad student Darwin. These women have fun helping each other with their knitting projects while supporting each other through life's difficulties.

Macomber, Debbie
The Shop on Blossom Street. Blossom Street Books. 2004. Mira. ISBN 0778320448. 352p.

In the first of the Blossom Street series, we meet cancer survivor Lydia, who owns a yarn shop, A Good Yarn. When she starts a knitting class, she forms special friendships and bonds with three women. Their first class project is a baby blanket. Jacqueline is hoping to disguises her dislike for her pregnant daughter-in-law by knitting one as a gift; Carol is hoping her IVF procedure will be successful; and Alix seems to be there just to serve her court-ordered community service project. Followed by *A Good Yarn* (2005) and *Back on Blossom Street* (2007).

Seitz, Rebecca
Prints Charming. **Sisters, Ink Series.** 2007. Westbow Press. ISBN 9781595542717. 320p.

Scrapbooking is the craft of choice in this Christian fiction entry. Jane and Lydia's friendship ended because Lydia didn't want to see her best friend make a mistake by marrying the wrong man. When Jane discovers her husband Bill is cheating on her, she gets a divorce and reconciles with Lydia. They decide to start Sisters, Ink, a scrapbooking business, making a new and diverse group of friends. When her ex tries to come crawling back, Jane learns to turn to her scrapbooking sisters to help her avoid making another huge mistake.

Snelling, Lauraine
The Healing Quilt. 2002. Waterbrook Press. ISBN 1578565383. 374p.

Three women become friends while making a quilt to raise money for a new hospital mammogram machine. Kit has recently lost her young daughter, Amber, to cancer, and she spearheads the project. Beth, married to a local pastor, desperately wants a baby after her miscarriage. Bossy Elaine finds a neighbor is causing her life to career out of control.

Working Women

She can bring home the bacon, fry it up in a pan, and never ever let him forget he's a man...

These novels mix work woes and women's lives.

Bagshawe, Louise
The Go-To Girl. 2005. St. Martin's Griffin. ISBN 0312339917. 372p.

London script reader Anna desperately wants to make it big in the film industry, but she's just too mousy to get ahead. She's not good at sucking up to the boss or flirting with the bigwigs. Having two supermodels as roommates isn't helping her confidence much, either. But when a hot new director uncovers her screenwriting talent, she may be on the way to bigger and better things.

Browne, Hester
Little Lady Agency. 2006. Pocket. ISBN 978–1416514923. 384p.

When serious and stable Melissa finds herself out of work and bored, she decides to start her own business, lending her skills to single men in need of those tasks only a woman can perform—picking out clothing, buying gifts, going to company parties. To keep her personal and professional lives separate she takes on a new persona, Honey, and becomes London's most sought-after bachelorette.

Burke, Betsy
Hardly Working. 2005. Red Dress Ink. ISBN 0373895429. 320p.

Dinah Nichols is a PR person for an environmental-protection agency. When the nonprofit's biggest contributor goes bankrupt, everyone is worried for their jobs. Dinah gets romantically involved with her boss, but will that help or hurt? Meanwhile, she's on the search for her unknown dad, who may be able to save the day.

Cabot, Meg
Boy Meets Girl. 2004. Avon. ISBN 0060085452. 387p.

Kate is a HR person at a NYC newspaper. When she has to fire someone unfairly, all hell breaks loose—she loses her job, gets sued, and ends up falling for the handsome lawyer representing her in the case. A crazy uptight boss, a stalker rocker ex-boyfriend, and funny family situations round out the comedy. Told as a series of emails, memos, and voice mails, this format works as a fast read that's a lot of fun.

Gold, Robin
⇨ *Perfectly True Tales of a Perfect Size 12.* 2007. Plume. ISBN 9780452288126. 272p.

Delilah White, an aspiring Martha Stewart, is up for a promotion that could make her a star. She's confident she'll get it—she's got personality, experience, and skills—but she finds herself thwarted at every turn by a rival determined to get the promotion herself at any cost. Scheming and sabotage abound in this funny story filled with appealing and realistic characters.

Holden, Wendy
Gossip Hound. 2003. Plume. ISBN 0452283930. 352p.

London book publicist Grace finds herself trapped in a job with a failing publisher. Adding to her troubles are a boring politician boyfriend and unaffectionate parents. When a major U.S. star hires her to promote his new book, she thinks her life is ready for a turnaround—until she reads the novel, that is. All of a sudden, her job becomes hell on earth. Witty and fun.

Van der Kwast, Jennifer
Pounding the Pavement. 2005. Broadway Books. ISBN 9780767919531. 288p.

After the film company she worked for goes bust, Sarah is looking for the perfect job but isn't really sure what that is. She meets an almost perfect guy. Meanwhile, her parents are bribing her to go to law school, her unemployment is about to run out, and she really wants to hold out for that perfect job. What's a single-in-the-city gal to do?

The Dating Game

There are winners and losers in the game of love, and these tales from the dating front put a funny spin on things.

Bird, Sarah
The Boyfriend School. 1989. Reprint, 2003, Ballantine. ISBN 9780345460097. 368p.

Photographer Gretchen is sent to cover the annual Luvboree, a romance writer's convention. There she meets Juanita and Lizzie, who think she needs to make over her love life. She decides that she can also be a romance writer but needs more romantic experiences to be able to write good scenes. Lizzie sets her up with her nerdy brother, whom Gretchen nicknames The Wisp, but he's quickly tossed aside as Gretchen becomes obsessed with a hunky mystery man. Clever and witty, with classic characters.

Bosnak, Karyn
⇨ *20 Times a Lady.* 2006. Harper. ISBN 9780060828356. 352p.

Delilah wakes up in bed with her boss. Not good for anyone, but this case is a bigger problem than you'd think: she had been fired the day before, and her boss, well, is kind of disgusting. Even worse, she has now hit her self-imposed limit of sleeping with 20 men. Going into overdrive on a quest for true love, Delilah tracks down her previous 19 conquests, convinced that she has to make it work with one of them. The results are absolutely hysterical—she embarks on a cross-country trek where she finds one in jail, one who has become a priest, and more than one who won't speak to her.

Cook, Claire
Must Love Dogs. 2002. Viking. ISBN 0670031062. 242p.

Divorced preschool teacher Sarah is getting pressured by her family to jump back into the dating pool. She grudgingly answers a personal ad, but her date turns out to be her widower father! Her sister writes Sarah an ad of her own, hoping for better results. As she goes through would-be suitors, her family sticks by her, hoping for a good match.

Curnyn, Linda
Confessions of an Ex Girlfriend. 2002. Red Dress Ink. ISBN 0373250150. 297p.

When her boyfriend sells a screenplay and moves from New York to Los Angeles, leaving her behind, Emma is thrust back into the world of dating. Her two best friends help her along, although they have romantic troubles of their own to deal with—one is considering cheating on her husband and the other has sworn off anything but casual sex. Fast paced and fun.

Frankel, Valerie
The Girlfriend Curse. 2005. Avon. ISBN 0060725540. 320p.

Peg is gaining a reputation as the girl you date before you find the girl you marry. Her last six boyfriends have all gotten engaged within six months after breaking up with her! Tired of the New York dating scene and determined to change her fate, she moves from Manhattan to rural Vermont, where she attends Inward Bound, a dating boot camp.

Harding, Robyn
Journal of Mortifying Moments. 2004. ISBN 034547628X. 304p.

In order to help her overcome her self-defeating dating habits, Kerry's therapist makes her write a journal of all the bad dates that have ever happened to her. These entries pop up against what's happening in her life now—she hates her ad agency job, her boyfriend's using her, and she decides to bring meaning into her life by mentoring an at-risk teen. Kerry's cringe-worthy journal entries are laugh-out-loud funny, and intersect nicely with the stories from her current search for fulfillment.

Graff, Laurie
You Have to Kiss a Lot of Frogs. 2004. Red Dress Ink. ISBN 0373250460. 443p.

At 45 and tired of attending bridal showers, New York City actress Karrie chronicles her dating life from the early 1990s to the present day. They're all here, from the guy who barked to the guy who wore the same outfit every day. Karrie's had a lot of dates, but why didn't she ever find true love? And is true love really necessary for a good life? Breezy, short chapter format makes this a light, fun read. Followed by *Looking for Mr. Goodfrog* (2006).

Moore, Jane
Love @ First Site. 2005. Broadway Books. ISBN 0767916905. 368p.

    Jess's pals sign her up for an internet dating service on her 34th birthday, with disastrous results. As she delves into the often bizarre world of online dating, Jess finds herself meeting men who stick her with the dinner bill, lie about their ages, income, and professions, and more. When her sister becomes ill, Jess starts to wonder whether her search for love has much meaning, and begins to reorganize her priorities.

Saunders, Kate
Bachelor Boys. 2005. St. Martin's. ISBN 0312339402. 304p.

    When Cassie's dear friend Phoebe, dying of leukemia, tells her she wants to see her two unruly sons married off before she dies, Cassie leaps into action. They aren't exactly great catches, however. Sensitive Ben is an unemployed musician, while rogue Fritz is an unemployed actor. And they're both much more interested in playing the field. But Cassie is determined to make Phoebe's final wish come true because warm and generous Phoebe has always been like a mother to her. She pulls out all of her best dating tricks to get the boys attached, with humorous results.

What Would You Do?

At one time or another, every one is faced with a choice that will shape the rest of their lives. Read these novels and ask yourself how the heroine's story would have turned out if she had taken a different turn.

Delinsky, Barbara
The Secret Between Us. 2007. Doubleday. ISBN 9780385518680. 352p.

    When Deborah's daughter Grace causes a car accident, injuring Grace's history teacher, Deborah sends Grace home and takes the blame herself. The next day, the man dies from his injuries, and the lie becomes a lot more serious. Grace is guilt ridden, Deborah risks losing everything, and secrets begin to come out about the teacher's past. An interesting look at how one impulsive moment can have long-reaching repercussions.

Giffin, Emily
Baby Proof. 2006. St. Martin's. ISBN 9780312348649. 352p.

    Claudia and Ben agreed that they didn't want to have children. After a few years of marriage though, one of their biological clocks starts ticking…and surprise, its Ben's. It doesn't help that their friends are all having babies, putting the pressure on Claudia. She decides that kids are a deal breaker and consents to a divorce despite being very much in love with her husband. Will either one give in?

Jackson, Joshilyn

Gods in Alabama. 2005. Warner. ISBN 0446524190. 288p.

When Arlene runs away from home she makes three promises to God—she will stop sleeping around, she will never tell another lie, and she will never return to Alabama. All He has to do in return is keep the body hidden. How's that for a premise? Then a former classmate comes knocking on her door looking for answers, and Arlene decides she needs to return home to do damage control. Once there, secrets come out of the woodwork and Arlene realizes that she might not be the only one involved in a young man's tragic end. Clever plot twists, with excellently drawn characters.

Packer, Ann

The Dive from Clausen's Pier. 2002. Knopf. ISBN 0375412824. 369p.

Carrie is about to break her engagement to Mike when he has a diving accident that leaves him paralyzed. Stricken with guilt and indecision, she spends the summer by his side but then runs away to New York City, where she discovers her talent for clothing design—plus a new romance. But will the pull of her friends and family force her off her new life track? An absorbing story about wonderful characters.

Schwarz, Christina

All is Vanity. 2002. Doubleday. ISBN 0385499728. 400p.

Margaret, a struggling author, begins to manipulate her best friend's life in order to get a good story out of her troubles. Letty recently moved to Los Angeles and is desperate to keep up appearances with her family's nouveau riche neighbors, so she's easily controlled by Margaret's suggestions to buy more, spend more, be more, even though she is plunging into debt and personal destruction. Margaret feels guilty, but is seduced by wanting to publish her book and tries to tell herself that her friend is responsible for her own actions. A fascinating look at the power we have over other people, the choices we make that may not be our own, and where lines get crossed.

Schwarz, Robin

⇨ *Night Swimming.* 2002. Warner. ISBN 0446532533. 252p.

Told she has one year left to live, Charlotte steals two million dollars from the bank she works at, fakes suicide, and runs away to Hollywood to assume a new identity. Along the way she falls in love, works on a "Things to Do Before I Die" list, and finds herself. Unfortunately, the cops back home are suspicious and start tracking her down. Very funny.

Winston, Lolly

Happiness Sold Separately. 2006. Warner. ISBN 0446533068. 304p.

Elinor and Ted's once-perfect marriage is rocked by infertility. Elinor's hormone treatments make her unhappy and withdrawn, and Ted finds solace in another woman. They decide to separate, not really sure if they want their marriage to end, but not sure if they are strong enough to weather infertility and infidelity. Meanwhile, Ted's new girlfriend knows that her young son may be her secret weapon in keeping their relationship going. Everyone's got a decision to make, and how it all ends may surprise you.

Second Chances

Everyone imagines a different life. Who wouldn't like to be someone else? What if these scenarios happened to you?

Colgan, Jenny

The Boy I Loved Before. 2004. St. Martin's Griffin. ISBN 0312331983. 320p.

At her best friend's wedding, Flora begins to regret her boring life and makes a wish that she could go back and have a do-over. The next morning, she wakes up as her 16-year-old self, but in the present, with one month to decide if she wants to stay a teenager or go back to her life.

Deveraux, Jude

Summerhouse. 2001. Pocket. ISBN 0671014188. 368p.

Three best friends who share the same birthday grapple with turning 40 while celebrating at a summerhouse in Maine. None of the women is happy with how her life turned out—Ellie is a successful author who lost every penny in a bad divorce, Madison gave up a promising modeling career to care for an ungrateful boyfriend, and Leslie is a dancer who left the stage for a boring suburban existence. When they meet up for their birthday festivities, a fortune-teller offers them the chance to go back in time to relive their lives. What a great birthday present!

Friedman, Elyse

Waking Beauty. 2004. Three Rivers Press. ISBN 1400051061. 244p.

A self-described "troll", Allison knows that the world doesn't like her simply because she's fat and unattractive. From her nasty roommate to her adoptive mother, people are mean and condescending. When she wakes up one day to discover that she is all of a sudden drop-dead gorgeous, it's funny how fast the world changes. Deciding to take her revenge for years of abuse, she comes to realize the importance of inner beauty. Wickedly funny.

Gaskell, Whitney

Good Luck. 2008. Bantam. ISBN 0553591517. 400p.

Lucy, a prep school teacher, is about to lose everything when a student falsely accuses her of sexual misconduct and she gets fired without a fair hearing. The day gets worse when she gets home to find her boyfriend in bed with another woman. However, things get a whole lot better when she realizes she's bought a winning lottery ticket—to the tune of $87 million. She heads to Palm Beach to escape her old life and start fresh, but can money really buy happiness?

Harmel, Kristin
The Blonde Theory. 2007. Hachette 5 Spot. ISBN 0446697590. 304p.

Overachieving lawyer Harper can't find a steady boyfriend. She out-earns most of her dates and intimidates the rest with her intellect. When her friends urge her to spend two weeks undercover as a ditzy blonde, she gives it a try, wearing skimpy outfits and playing down her intelligence. It's not easy, and she ends up with disastrous results. Her social calendar quickly fills up, but all of the men she attracts are simply interested in casual sex. Who says blondes have more fun?

Heller, Jane
Infernal Affairs. 1996. Kensington. ISBN 1575660210. 295p.

Overweight, prematurely gray, and unhappy, Barbara is at the end of her rope when her husband tells her he wants a divorce. After drowning her sorrows, she stumbles out into a storm, begging the heavens for a new life. Surprise, she wakes up the next morning with a playmate's body, shining blonde hair, and a huge upswing in luck. What's the catch? Well, it seems she's made a deal with the devil, who expects a lot in return.

Henry, April
Learning to Fly. 2002. Thomas Dunne. ISBN 0312290527. 308p.

Free Meeker is tired of her hippie family, cheating boyfriend, and dead-end job, so she takes a road trip to visit her sister in Oregon. She gets involved in a huge car accident on the way home, which kills her hitchhiker passenger, a runaway wife. When she finds herself listed among the dead and comes across a bag containing a huge sum of money, Free takes the opportunity to assume the woman's identity. Turns out that wasn't such a good idea. While this book is not usually classified as women's fiction, Free's back story and struggle for identity are firmly underlying the suspense.

Kinsella, Sophie
Remember Me? 2008. Dial Press. ISBN 9780385338721. 384p.

After a nasty bump to the head, Lexi wakes up in a hospital room, unable to remember the past three years of her life. She can't recall a single thing about her glamorous life—not her rich husband, mind-boggling home, or new set of friends. When she looks in the mirror, she doesn't even recognize herself—how did she get those teeth, that body, that hair? When her lost memory begins to cause her life to unravel, causing problems at work, bringing up drama with old friends, and shocking her with the discovery of a supposed lover, she has to decide which life she really wants—her new ultra-glam one or her old comfortable one from three years earlier.

Michaels, Fern
Pretty Woman. 2005. Pocket. ISBN 0743457811. 329p.

>   Rosie runs a successful mail-order business, and is well aware that her husband Kent only married her for her money. When she finally decides to kick him out, she hopes for a nice turnaround in her life. What she isn't expecting is to win the lottery—$302 million—that same night. Determined for a makeover, she tries to keep Kent away and embarks on a personal training routine—with a hot trainer, of course.

Monroe, Mary Alice
Girl in the Mirror. 1998. Mira. ISBN 1551664518. 442p.

>   Charlotte has been horribly disfigured since birth. When a settlement from a lawsuit brings her a large sum of money, she decides to have extreme plastic surgery, getting a new jaw and an entirely new face. All of a sudden, she's a sought-after Hollywood star, leading a life she never dreamed was possible Then her body begins to reject the implants. Will Charlotte lose everything?

Scotch, Allison Winn
Time of My Life: A Novel. 2008. Shaye Areheart Books. ISBN 0307408574. 288p.

>   Jillian appears to have the perfect suburban life. A fabulous home in Westchester County, New York; a successful lawyer husband named Henry; and a beautiful baby girl. Yet for some reason, she can't help constantly wondering, "What if?" After learning that her post-college boyfriend, Jackson, is engaged, she wishes she could go back and see what might have been. And then she wakes up—seven years in the past. Pre-Henry, pre-baby, still living in a cramped Manhattan apartment with Jackson. Now that she has the chance to revisit her life, will things change?

Smolinski, Jill
⇨ *Next Thing on My List.* 2006. Shaye Areheart Books. ISBN 9780307351241. 304p.

>   June offers Marisa, a complete stranger, a ride home from their Weight Watchers meeting. They get into a car accident, and Marisa dies—leaving behind a list of 20 Things to Do by My 25th Birthday, which June decides to complete for her. She discovers that following Marisa's list gives her life the purpose and direction she had been looking for. Charming, sentimental, and humorous.

Soap Operas

Sometimes a bit hard to believe, sometimes overly dramatic, sometimes full of sadness, these titles are always a good read to get involved in, just like a good TV soap opera.

Delinsky, Barbara

➪ *Family Tree.* 2006. Doubleday. ISBN 9780385518659. 368p.

Dana knew it would be a difficult transition into her husband Hugh's esteemed New England family. After all, she doesn't even know her real father, while the Clarkes can trace their lineage back to the Mayflower. When the couple's first baby has distinctly African American coloring and features, suspicions and accusations abound. Was Dana cheating on Hugh? Does this have something to do with her unknown father? Or was one of Hugh's relatives getting a little something on the side? An engrossing look at issues of race, family, and trust.

Fielding, Joy

Grand Avenue. 2001. Pocket. ISBN 0743407075. 392p.

Four women meet at their children's playground in the 1970s and remain friends for the next 20-odd years. Each woman's life holds a story—Chris deals with an abusive husband; beauty queen Barbara becomes obsessed with youth and her looks; Susan deals with sexual harassment at work; and workaholic Vicki climbs the ladder of professional success at the expense of her family and friends. A saga of four lives worthy of any daytime Emmy.

Fowler, Therese

Souvenir. 2008. Ballantine. ISBN 9780345499684. 384p.

Meg and Carson grew up on neighboring farms, and seemed destined to be together. However, right before Carson was set to propose, Meg announced her engagement to the son of the town's banker, much to everyone's shock. Marrying money saved the family farm, so she never looked back; but 15 years later, Carson has become a huge rock star, and Meg is trapped in a loveless marriage with a teenage daughter who just might be Carson's. When Meg discovers she has ALS (Lou Gehrig's Disease), she decides it's time to make peace with the past. A juicy subplot involving her daughter's online romance with an older boy provides just enough spark to keep this from descending into tear-jerker territory.

Fulton, Eileen

Soap Opera. 1999. St. Martin's. ISBN 0312203659. 311p.

After being left at the altar, Amanda heads to New York, determined to make it big on Broadway. But instead of hoofing the floorboards, she lands a stint as a long-lost daughter on *Another Life,* a long-running soap opera, because she's a dead ringer for one of the stars. Then her life begins to strangely mirror soap opera plots—thanks to losing her virginity the night before her non-wedding, she finds out she's pregnant, and her ex shows up on her doorstep begging to be rescued from debt. Frothy fun.

Goudge, Eileen

The Second Silence. 2000. Viking. ISBN 0670891592. 365p.

Recovering alcoholic Noelle decides she needs to divorce her sleazy and domineering husband, Robert. That doesn't go over well with him, so he drugs her and snatches their five-year-old daughter Emma, intending to paint Noelle as an unfit mother. Noelle seeks the assistance of her family, who all have their own demons to confront. Layered and fast paced.

Michael, Judith
The Real Mother. 2005. William Morrow. ISBN 0060599294. 304p.

When her stepfather disappears and her mother has a stroke, Sarah gives up medical school to return home to Chicago and take care of her three younger siblings. When her long-lost older half-brother Mack returns as well, she's resentful and untrusting. What's his agenda? Meanwhile, a budding romance with a mysterious client starts to complicate life as well, and when her beau's ex comes out of the woodwork, what's her agenda? And how is she connected to Mack? Just over-the-top enough to satisfy.

Michaels, Fern
About Face. 2003. Zebra Books. ISBN 0821770209. 381p.

Casey is released from a mental institution after 10 years of memory loss. She returns to the home of her mother, desperate to unravel the secrets of her past. Turns out she was abused by her stepbrother, neglected by mum, and why doesn't anyone in her hometown want anything to do with her? A gorgeous doctor comes to her rescue but someone is determined to keep the skeletons firmly in the closet.

Milestone Birthdays

Some people really find milestone birthdays (such as 30th, 40th, 60th, etc.) to be hard. These women deal with life's transitions in different ways—some with humor, some with grace, some with drama.

Castoro, Laura
A New Lu. 2005. Red Dress Ink. ISBN 0373895143. 391p.

On the eve of her 50th birthday, magazine columnist Lu is embroiled in a midlife crisis. She works for *Five-O,* a magazine targeted to her age group, and her boss wants her to endure a total makeover in order to chronicle the changes in her column. Lu's in for a really extreme makeover, however, when a last fling with her soon-to-be ex-husband leaves her pregnant. Lu was ready for the change of life, but this is a bit more of a change than she was expecting.

Clare, Lucy
Hoping for Hope. 2002. Dutton. ISBN 0525946373. 294p.

The week she turns 50 is the worst week of Liddy's life. As if dealing with such a milestone birthday wasn't stressful enough, she also finds out that her husband is cheating on her, she gets fired from her job, and whoops—it's not menopause—she's pregnant. And the baby is not her husband's. As everyone in her family has an opinion on what to do about the baby, Liddy must make some serious choices and finally take control of her life.

Gaskell, Whitney
Pushing 30. 2003. Bantam. ISBN 0553382241. 326p.

Good girl Ellie seems to have a great life—she's an attorney in Washington, D.C., with a sassy best friend and a great boyfriend. As she approaches 30 though, life starts to take a distinct downturn. She loses her job, breaks up with her boyfriend, and her mother is about to drive her off the deep end. Things start to look up when a potential new beau comes on the scene, but then she realizes he's twice her age—and she's already feeling old herself. What does that make him, then?

Gruenenfelder, Kim
⇨ *A Total Waste of Makeup.* 2005. St. Martin's. ISBN 031234872X. 384p.

Charlize enjoys her job as a personal assistant to a hot male movie star, but as her 30th birthday looms, she finds herself wanting more out of life. Her family is driving her nuts, acting as her younger sister's maid of honor makes her feel old, and her best friend and her boss are becoming romantically involved. Convinced that she'll never have children of her own, she writes advice in a journal to pass on to a future grandniece and realizes she knows a lot more than she gives herself credit for—and that 30 isn't so bad after all.

Hunt, Diane
Hot Flashes and Cold Cream. 2006. Thomas Nelson. ISBN 1595540695. 320p.

Maggie, just about to turn 50, is on the brink of a midlife crisis. Her husband has a cute new secretary, her children have left the nest, and everything in the mirror is sagging. When a former high school classmate fails to recognize her, she decides it's high time to make some changes. When Maggie meets an older neighbor, the eccentric and evangelizing Lily, she realizes that perhaps there is more to life than what is on the surface. Light Christian fare with a good sense of humor.

Ironside, Virginia
No! I Don't Want to Join a Book Club: Diary of a Sixtieth Year. 2007. Viking. ISBN 9780670038183. 240p.

About to turn 60, Marie looks forward to relaxing and being comfortable, unlike some of her friends, who want to take up hang gliding or go on African safaris. She's also excited about her new grandson and sees no reason to want to reclaim her youth. But when her dear friend Hugh is diagnosed with a fatal disease, she realizes she doesn't want to get too comfortable; and she decides to seek out an old crush.

Porter, Jane
Flirting with 40. 2006. Hachette 5 Spot. ISBN 9780446697262. 356p.

Facing her 40th birthday, Jackie contends with becoming a single mom of two when her husband leaves her. Depressed, she and a pal book a trip to

Hawaii, but when the friend backs out at the last minute, Jackie goes it alone. There she falls for a handsome surf instructor and makes several subsequent trips back to the islands to meet up with him, torn between the fantasy life she can experience in Hawaii and the drudgery of home as a single 40 year old. When family issues come to a head, she must decide the direction she really wants her life to take.

Snow, Carol
Getting Warmer. 2007. Berkley. ISBN 0425213544. 336p.

Natalie, a high school teacher living with her parents in Scottsdale, Arizona, is approaching her 30th birthday. She's stuck at home thanks to her bad debts and her mother's illness. To meet men, she and her girlfriends spin huge lies about their backgrounds and lives, which works until she meets a man she actually wants to see more than once. Will she finally grow up and be able to have a real relationship?

Webb, Sarah
Always the Bridesmaid. 2004. Avon. ISBN 0060571667. 352p.

Dublin bookseller Amy dreads her upcoming 30th birthday, especially since she's tired of being single. It comes to a head when she discovers that her best friend is sleeping with her ex, her sister and her best friend announce that they're both getting married, and they both want Amy to be their bridesmaid.

The Big Transition

These coming-of-age novels weave wonderful stories of maturing young women.

Bank, Melissa
The Wonder Spot. 2005. Viking. ISBN 0670034118. 336p.

Sophie, a witty, self-deprecating suburban child, grows up into an astute young woman. Over the course of 20 years she struggles to define herself throughout Hebrew school, college, and her first job. Her family plays a big role in the story as well, from her grandmother's descent into senility, her quiet father and high-strung mother, and her two brothers.

Blume, Judy
Summer Sisters. 1998. Delacorte. ISBN 0385324057. 400p.

Caitlin and Vix are "summer sisters," meeting up every vacation in New England. Caitlin is wealthy and beautiful, while Vix comes from a poor, troubled home. They grow up together over several summers, testing the limits and strengthening their intense bond. After high school, Caitlin becomes a world traveler and can't understand why Vix can't leave her Harvard scholarship to join her. Blume explores 18 years in the lives of two women and the lasting effects of their relationship.

Brashares, Ann
The Last Summer of You and Me. 2007. Riverhead Books. ISBN 9781594489174. 320p.

Shy, sweet Alice and her headstrong, sporty sister Riley come of age at their summer house on Fire Island, along with their best friend, Paul. Both girls are childlike in different ways—Alice is naïve while Riley is something of a female Peter Pan. Paul and Alice have a secret, strong attachment growing, while Riley shuns any talk of romance. When Riley becomes seriously ill, childlike Alice is torn between her conflicting feelings for Paul and loyalty to her sister and realizes they all need to finally grow up.

Fitch, Janet
White Oleander. 1999. Little, Brown. ISBN 0316569321. 390p.

Astrid, 13, is bounced around through the foster care system after her flighty mother is sent to prison. Her first foster mother is Starr, a born-again former abuser, whose middle-aged boyfriend seduces Astrid. When Starr finds out, her jealous rage leads her to send Astrid to her next foster home, with the tyrannical Marvel, and from there to the sadistic and neglectful Amelia. When she finally lands with a "dream" family, yuppie couple Claire and Ron, there is trouble in that home as well, manipulated by Iris. How Astrid gets through her ordeals and grows up into a mature young woman makes for an absorbing read.

McCandless, Sarah Grace
Grosse Pointe Girl: Tales from a Suburban Adolescence. 2004. Simon & Schuster. ISBN 0743256123. 192p.

Set in a wealthy Michigan suburb in the 1980s, this story follows Emma from the summer before sixth grade to her high school graduation. Emma goes through typical adolescent rites of passage, such as getting her first bra, being bullied by the popular girls, experiencing unrequited love, getting fake IDs, and adjusting to her parents' separation. Told as episodic reflections in the first person, this is a quick and enjoyable read that will appeal to anyone who grew up in the era of Madonna and Michael Jackson.

Simons, Paullina
⇨ *Tully.* 1994. St. Martin's. ISBN 0312110839. 594p.

The bond between three teenage girls forms the core of this sprawling, absorbing novel. Abused by her mentally ill mother and her uncle, Tully barely survives her wretched adolescence in 1970s Kansas. Julie, who comes from a large Hispanic family, is determined to do better for herself. And Jenny, moderately autistic, wants to escape her overprotective parents. As the three unlikely friends struggle against their origins and circumstances, their lives take uncharted paths marked by both destiny and choice.

Sittenfeld, Curtis
The Man of My Dreams. 2006. Random House. ISBN 1400064767. 288p.

Hannah's story begins at age 14, as she is living with her aunt after her parent's messy divorce. Emotionally stunted, Hannah gets through college without forming a single lasting relationship. Her only female friend is her cousin, Fig, who takes advantage of her at every opportunity. Boyfriends only break her heart, if she lets them get close enough. When at age 28 she finally she confronts her domineering father, she must come to terms with her past in order to forge ahead with her future.

It's Beginning to Look a lot like Christmas

Heartwarming, fun tales for the holiday season.

Andrews, Mary Kay
Blue Christmas. 2006. HarperCollins. ISBN 0060837349. 208p.

Antiques dealer Weezie's holiday fun keeps getting sabotaged. She's fervently working to get her shop ready for the holidays but mysterious break-ins to her home, truck, and shop keep her busy—and upset. Oddly enough, the only things missing are quirky display pieces and trays of party food. To make matters worse, her boyfriend's sour attitude is ruining any chance of a merry time. Breezy and fun, no typical holiday schmaltz here.

Chiaverini, Jennifer
The Christmas Quilt. **Elm Creek Quilts Series.** 2005. Simon & Schuster. ISBN 074328657X. 206p.

While searching for decorations on Christmas Eve, Sarah finds a lovely unfinished Christmas quilt. Elm Creek master quilter Sylvia knows the quilt's history and narrates several tales of holidays past. Memories and family secrets unfold as Sylvia recalls how many times the quilt had been pulled out of storage to be completed, only to be forgotten as drama unfolded and then put away for next year.

Frank, Dorothea Benton
The Christmas Pearl. 2007. HarperCollins. ISBN 0061438448. 176p.

In a holiday season filled with all slice-and-bake cookies, Internet gift certificates, and bickering family members throwing insults, 93-year old Theodora becomes lost in memories of past holidays. The family's strict housekeeper, Pearl, would overdecorate, overcook, and have long fireside chats with her. When Theodora is about to give up, the spirit of Pearl appears and smoothes over the holiday for all. A charming read that includes holiday recipes.

Hill, Donna, and Francis Ray
Rockin' Around that Christmas Tree. 2003. St. Martin's. ISBN 0312321953. 152p.

Everyone likes to think of Denise as a dependable, gentle, upper-class African American housewife. When her husband demands that she give up her dream of opening a sewing and design shop, she bucks her carefully constructed persona and announces her plans for divorce during Thanksgiving dinner, putting her whole family at odds. As Christmas approaches, will she have struck out on her own, or renew the family bond?

Naman, Christine Pisera
Christmas Lights. 2007. Doubleday. ISBN 9780385522458. 128p.

Seven different women deal with the holiday, with each getting a chapter for her story. Katherine is caring for her sick husband; Adrianna is working through a difficult marriage; Isabella is going to be a new mother. The last vignette reveals how these women and four more are connected. A nice gentle read.

Roberts, Sheila
⇨ *On Strike for Christmas.* 2007. St. Martin's. ISBN 9780312370220. 352p.

Laura is fed up with doing everything around the house while her husband watches TV. Joy is tired of giving in to her grumpy husband while never getting to do what she wants. To teach their husbands a lesson, they decide to go on strike for Christmas. The members of their knitting club eagerly join in, and soon enough the newspaper picks up the story. All of a sudden women all over town are on strike, leaving the harried husbands in charge of everything, with hysterical results. Fun and festive.

Thayer, Nancy
Hot Flash Holidays. **Hot Flash Club Series.** 2005. Ballantine. ISBN 0345485513. 304p.

The Hot Flash Club is celebrating the holidays at The Haven, an exclusive spa. Unfortunately, the holiday cheer only goes so far when each of the ladies realizes what's on her plate for the season. Polly sets her house on fire trying to please her family, Faye breaks her ankle, Shirley makes a big financial mistake involving her much younger boyfriend, and they all seem to have man issues. Throughout the year to the following Christmas, the ladies band together to solve their problems. Humorous and light.

The Grand Dames of Story

No book on women's fiction titles would be complete without the addition of the master storytellers. Although some readers could quibble—are they romance authors, women's fiction writers, or just story-churning machines?—there's no question that readers consider them a classic part of the women's fiction oeuvre.

Bradford, Barbara Taylor
A Woman of Substance. 1979. Doubleday. ISBN 0385120508. 759p.
Just Rewards. 2006. St. Martin's. ISBN 0312307063. 496p.

The ultimate rags-to-riches saga. The Harte Family series begins with *A Woman of Substance,* in which Emma Harte rises from poverty to become the head the world's most famous department store. Along the way she handles rakes, takeover plots, and feuds. The final entry in the six-book series, *Just Rewards,* finds Emma's great-granddaughters confronting marriages, rivalries, and the intricacies of the family business. Any of Bradford's 30-plus sagas are sure bets for entertainment and strong female characters.

Brown, Sandra
In a Class by Itself. 1984. Reprint, 1999, Bantam. ISBN 0553104136.
The Witness. 1995. Warner. ISBN 0446603309. 422p.

Brown, author of over 70 novels, started out writing paperback romances and moved into romantic suspense territory. *In a Class by Itself* is the sweetly romantic story of Dani and Logan, high school sweethearts who meet again at their 10th reunion. They had eloped but Dani's parents intervened, spirited her away, and had the marriage annulled. Logan never understood why she never came back to him, and now that she's back and needs a favor, he's determined to get what he wants—an explanation and her commitment. *The Witness* is a taut and twisting thriller featuring district attorney Kendall Deaton, who risks her life and that of her infant son to testify against her ex-husband, a violent white supremacist, and his father. Amnesia, murder, romance, and danger abound in this page-turner.

Cookson, Catherine
Kate Hannigan. 1950. MacDonald. Reprint, 2008, Corgi. ISBN 0552156728. 400p.
Kate Hannigan's Girl. 2001. Simon & Schuster. ISBN 0743212525. 288p.

Cookson, a master of the women's saga, brought rich settings and spirited and likeable characters to life in her 100 novels. Her first, *Kate Hannigan,* is the story of a young woman living at the turn of the 20th century. A shunned single mother, her inner strength and intelligence help her rise above the poverty she was born into. Her final novel, published 50 years later, follows Kate's daughter, Annie, who has spent her life struggling with the stigma of illegitimacy and now wishes to join a convent. Cookson mixes romance, class struggle, and history in her lush and well-written stories.

Roberts, Nora
Birthright. 2003. Putnam. ISBN 0399149848. 464p.
Tribute. 2008. Putnam. ISBN 0399154914. 488p.

Robert's books are too numerous to keep track of, and they range from historical to contemporary, from steamy to suspenseful. She even writes a hybrid mystery-futuristic-romance series under the name J. D. Robb. In *Birthright,* she tells the story of Callie, an archaeologist who uncovers a family she never knew she had. Toss in a murder, family secrets, and romance, and you've got all the plot you need. *Tribute* is a softer, more romantic tale with subtle suspense. Cilla is restoring her grandmother Janet's estate. Janet, a famous movie star, died under mysterious circumstances in the 1950s, and Cilla discovers a collection of unsigned love letters, leading to much suspicion and drama.

Steel, Danielle
⇨ *Granny Dan.* 1999. Delacorte. ISBN 0385317093. 223p.
The Klone and I. 1998. Delacorte. ISBN 0385323921. 232p.

A veritable writing machine, Steel has given us 80-plus novels varied in setting, characters, and story. But all feature women triumphing over some adversity (from slight to dramatic) and most often, finding love. In *Granny Dan,* Steel leaves her usual contemporary setting to tell a tale that moves from czarist Russia to modern-day Vermont. Danina is a talented ballerina with the St. Petersburg ballet until she is stricken with influenza just as the Russian revolution looms. When the handsome doctor she falls in love with sends her off to his relatives in America, her life is forever changed. In the completely different *The Klone and I,* Steel delves into the futuristic world of cloning. Newly divorced Stephanie travels to Paris and meets a handsome scientist who has cloned himself. She falls in love with him and must decide between the real man and his clone. Wacky and unusual, yet charming.

The World Will Never Be the Same Again: Life During Wartime

The novels showcased here cover a range of historical time periods—World War I, World War II, Vietnam, and the 9/11 terrorist attacks—but they all feature the same themes of love, loss, and lives forever changed by war.

Berg, Elizabeth
Dream When You're Feeling Blue. 2007. Random House. ISBN 1400065100. 256p.

Three Chicago sisters—Kitty, Louise, and Tish—learn what it means to make sacrifices during wartime. Every evening the sisters get together to write letters to their men—Louise to her fiancé in Europe, Kitty to the man fighting in the Pacific whom she wishes was her fiancé, and Tish to a variety of young men she meets at USO dances. The letters the sisters send and receive are intimate glimpses of life both on the battlefront and at home.

Colin, Beatrice
⇨ *The Glimmer Palace.* 2008. Riverhead. ISBN 1594489858. 400p.

Lilly Nelly Aphrodite grows up in a Berlin orphanage in the early 20th century. As the novel progresses, she endures tough times during World War I through the rise of the Nazis at the dawn of World War II. Narrowly escaping the life of prostitution that her best friend Hanne succumbs to, she eventually becomes a leading film star. Vividly portraying the intense poverty, disgruntlement, and general emptiness of life between the wars in Europe, this is a powerful portrait of a strong-willed young woman struggling to survive in a harsh world.

Dann, Patty
Sweet & Crazy. 2003. St. Martin's. ISBN 0312316666. 193p.

Hanna, a creative writing teacher, struggles to raise her young son post-9/11. Widowed shortly before that fateful September, they live in a small town in Ohio, which quickly goes from quaint and friendly to racist and untrusting. Suddenly family friends of Indian descent are mistaken for Arabic and harassed, while Hanna herself receives threats for her Jewish heritage. A thoughtful tale of loss and renewal.

Gilchrist, Ellen
A Dangerous Age. 2008. Algonquin. ISBN 1565125428. 256p.

Three cousins face important personal decisions in the aftermath of the 9/11 terrorist attacks. Winnie has lost her fiancé in the World Trade Center collapse, and moves to Washington, D.C., to live with her cousin Louise, a high-powered TV executive. The two women find themselves dating twin Marines who have emotional and physical scars from the war in Afghanistan. Their other cousin, Olivia, struggles with doubt when her husband is called to active duty in Iraq.

McDermott, Alice
After This. 2006. Farrar, Straus, and Giroux. ISBN 0374168091. 288p.

The Keane family deals with the many changes happening in American in the1960s, from the sexual revolution to the controversy of the Vietnam War. John and Mary meet shortly after World War II, get married, and raise their conventional, middle-class family on Long Island, confronting the social and religious struggles of the times. This episodic novel uses flashbacks and foreshadowing to delve into a family growing up together in a changing world.

McMullan, Margaret
In My Mother's House. 2003. Thomas Dunne. ISBN 0312318243. 262p.

Jenny de Bazsi was a schoolgirl during World War II when her Jewish family escaped the Nazis in Vienna, immigrated to Chicago, and converted to Catholicism—a part of her life she'd like to forget. Her grown daughter Elizabeth is fascinated with the past, however, and becomes obsessed with pressing her mother for details of the war years. Mother and daughter must confront ugly truths in this family saga.

Schwartz, Lynne Sharon
The Writing on the Wall: A Novel. 2005. Counterpoint. ISBN 1582432996. 304p.

Renata, a librarian in New York City, has endured plenty of trauma in her 34 years. Her twin sister drowns under suspicious circumstances shortly

after giving birth at age 16; her father died and her mother was institutional-
ized soon after; and Renata was left to raise her niece, who was kidnapped.
It's no surprise that she has built a thick shell around her heart and trusts no
one. Days after the Twin Towers are hit, Renata finds herself in charge of
another child, the son of her boyfriend's secretary, who perished in the collapse. The novel evokes the deep shock suffered by New Yorkers in the wake
of the attacks, from the constant TV coverage to the searches for missing
loved ones, while focusing on the troubled Renata, striving for a normal
family life.

Shields, Jody
The Crimson Portrait. 2006. Little, Brown. ISBN 0316785288. 304p.
>Catherine loses her husband in World War I and honors his wish to have
their English estate turned into an army hospital. She continues to live on the
property and becomes obsessed with a severely disfigured patient, Julian, who
reminds her of her dead husband. Richly drawn, this novel recreates desperate
times and desperate people trying to survive the war.

Sullivan, Faith
Gardenias. 2005. Milkweed Editions. ISBN 1571310452. 380p.
>Leaving an abusive husband, Arlene, her sister Betty, and her young
daughter Lark move to California in 1942 to establish new lives for themselves
and to find work in the war plants. Told from Lark's point of view, the novel
follows the three through struggles and joys living in a housing project in San
Diego during the bleak years of World War II.

In Sickness and in Health:
Women Dealing with Illness

Illnesses of any type can be difficult to manage. Whether relying on strong
friendships, loved ones, or simply relying on one's own strong will, these novels feature heroines dealing with illness in many ways—some with sadness,
some with humor, and all with grace.

Albert, Elisa
The Book of Dahlia: A Novel. 2008. Free Press. ISBN 0743291298. 288p.
>Dahlia, a pot-smoking, unemployed slacker, is diagnosed with a terminal
brain tumor at age 29. She endures seizures, grueling radiation treatments, and
a support group. She comes across a lightweight self-help book called *It's Up
to You: Your Cancer To-Do List,* and tries to live by it's principles, but her
bitter sense of humor and anger at the universe prevent her from accepting her
illness. Sometimes harsh, sometimes humorous, this is a decidedly non-weepy
look at cancer.

Hilderbrand, Elin
Barefoot: A Novel. 2007. Little, Brown. ISBN 0316018589. 416p.

Vicki, an "alpha mom" diagnosed with lung cancer, has packed up her family to spend the summer in Nantucket. Her sister Brenda and best friend Melanie join her, ostensibly to help care for Vicki's two young sons while she is in chemotherapy, but the two women are unprepared for the task, each absorbed in their own problems—Brenda has been fired from her teaching job for having an affair with a student, while Melanie has left her cheating husband even though she's pregnant. At the heart of the story though is Vicki's battle with cancer and her emotional rollercoaster as she prepares to die.

Michna, Tanya
Necessary Arrangements. 2007. NAL Accent. ISBN 0451222075. 314p.

Asia Swenson's breast cancer returns just as her family is preparing for her younger sister's wedding. As Asia struggles to fight the disease, she also must make accommodations for the rest of her life—putting her career on hold, trying to do her best as the maid of honor for her sister, and nurturing a blossoming romance with a coworker. Humor, dynamic and realistic characters, and the bond between the sisters make this a touching read.

Mitchard, Jacquelyn
The Breakdown Lane. 2005. HarperCollins. ISBN 0060587245. 400p.

Leo abandons Julianne, his wife of 20 years, to live on a commune. She's left with no money and two teenagers—one of them learning disabled—the other a toddler. Added to her woes is a diagnosis of multiple sclerosis. The deterioration of Julie's health is heart-wrenching and realistic. This could have easily become a weepy disease-of-the-month novel, but Mitchard tackles illness, abandonment, and family issues with grace.

Orloff, Erica
Do They Wear High Heels in Heaven? 2005. Red Dress Ink. ISBN 0373895356. 248p.

On a newspaper assignment for Breast Cancer Awareness Month, New York journalist Lily gets a mammogram, thinking she will just "get her breasts smashed and write about it." You guessed it, the doctor discovers a lump. Lily has two children to worry about, so she turns to her best friend, Michael, to be their guardian when she's gone. A serious subject approached with warmth and humor.

Riley, Jess
⇨ *Driving Sideways.* 2008. Ballantine. ISBN 0345501101. 342p.

In this laugh-out-loud road trip novel, 28-year-old Leigh is traveling across the country to visit the family of her organ donor. Living with kidney disease since she was a teen, Leigh has always been a homebody, carefully choosing her next steps. Since her transplant, she's been trying all kinds of new things and decides to throw caution to the wind to set out on an adventure. Along the way she meets some interesting characters and starts to feel the effects of a possible relapse. Witty dialogue, fun characters, and an adventurous plot mark this debut novel, which also puts an interesting spotlight on living with a chronic disease and the aftermath of organ transplantation.

Scotch, Allison Winn
The Department of Lost and Found. 2007. William Morrow. ISBN 0061161411. 320p.

Natalie, a young, ambitious senior aide to a senator from New York, is ditched by her cheating boyfriend right after she's diagnosed with breast cancer. As if that weren't enough, she loses her job soon after, and finds her carefully cultivated world falling apart. People aren't who she thought they were, her ambition fades as her treatment program gets harder, and she doesn't know what to do next or who to turn to. Natalie's battle with cancer is portrayed with humor and grace, and the story also deftly portrays a young woman surviving a terrible illness and growing as a person post-cancer.

Walker, Laura Jensen
Reconstructing Natalie. 2006. WestBow Press. ISBN 9781595540676. 320p.

After Natalie is diagnosed with breast cancer at age 27, her boyfriend breaks up with her, some of her friends start avoiding her, and she even feels left out of her church. Luckily her family stands by her, and she makes new friends. Natalie goes through chemotherapy, a mastectomy, and reconstructive surgery. An enjoyable sense of humor lightens a serious topic.

Note

1. James Baldwin, quoted in Jerome Agel and Walter D. Glanze, *Pearls of Wisdom: A Harvest of Quotations from All Ages* (New York: HarperCollins, 1987), 97.

Chapter Two

Character

One of the strongest appeal factors of women's fiction is character. Readers love to see themselves reflected in the story, or they enjoy recognizing characters who may be just like their friends. Sometimes it's the opposite, and we like to read about the kinds of women we'd never be (in good ways and in bad!).

This does not mean that women's fiction characters are stock, however. Indeed, it means that there are as many different characters as there are different types of women in the world. The lists in this chapter group together similar characters of a wide variety. While the plots or pacing may not be the same within the lists, the characters are a constant. You'll meet actresses, Southern belles, mothers, widows, women of different races and backgrounds, and more.

Like Mother, Like Daughter

The mother–daughter relationship is one of the most tenuous of all relationships. Can we ever get away from turning into our mothers?

Berg, Elizabeth
What We Keep. 1998. Random House. ISBN 0375500995. 272p.
   Ginny and Sharla haven't seen their mother, Marion, in 35 years. Marion abandoned the preteen girls in order to find herself and pursue an art career. Now hinting that she has cancer, Marion gets the sisters to visit her and put the past to rest. Berg has a knack for giving plenty of insight into the emotions and dreams of her richly drawn characters.

French, Wendy

sMothering. 2003. Forge. ISBN 0765307936. 301p.

What do you do when your overbearing and critical mother drops by ... and stays? Claire is not happy when her domineering mother comes by for an unexpected and open-ended visit. Between trying to find a boyfriend, pressures at work, unreliable pals, and now this, she pretty much has a breakdown. Of course, Mom has problems of her own, and mother and daughter come to realize they can help each other through life's little crises. A fun, chick lit take on mothers and daughters.

Gaffney, Patricia

Circle of Three. 2000. HarperCollins. ISBN 0060193751. 421p.

Recently widowed, Carrie struggles to raise her teenage daughter, Ruth. It doesn't help that just before her husband died, he moved the family back to the town Carrie grew up in—and couldn't wait to escape. Carrie's disapproving mother, Dana, stopped her from marrying the man she really loved. And guess what? He still lives in town. Problem is, now it's Carrie's daughter who wants to stop the relationship. Told in alternating voices, Gaffney's look at the tenuous connections between three generations of women.

Lipman, Elinor

Then She Found Me. 1990. Pocket. Reprint 2008, Washington Square Press. ISBN 9781416589938. 320p.

When 36-year-old April's adoptive parents die, her birth mother shows up out of nowhere. Brassy Bernice, a local TV talk show host, intends to publicly creating a mother–daughter relationship with April. The two women are as different as night and day, and April never really had any curiosity about her birth mom to begin with. A wry and moving portrait of an instant family.

Pietrzyk, Leslie

⇨ *A Year and a Day.* 2004. Morrow. ISBN 0060554657. 351p.

Suffering from depression, Annette, the mother of 15-year-old Alice, commits suicide. A few days later, Alice begins to hear her mother's voice, giving her advice. As the year moves on, Annette reveals her secrets to her daughter, and Alice spends time figuring out the world around her and just where she fits in to it. Pietrzyk's quirky novel tackles what could have been a morbid or overly sentimental subject with light humor and wonderful characters.

Sebold, Alice

The Almost Moon. 2007. Little, Brown. ISBN 0316003611. 304p.

Helen resents her duty as caretaker for her senile mother, Clair. One evening, having had it with the stress and tediousness, she suffocates Clair and then doesn't quite know how to cope with the aftermath. Helen unravels the story of her life and her mother's descent into mental illness. The relationship between Helen her mother unravels at a slow pace but gives the reader much insight into how it turned Helen into the person she has become.

Shelton, Sandi Kahn
What Comes After Crazy. 2005. Shaye Areheart. ISBN 1400082951. 320p.

Maz grew up in the shadow of her mother, the sexy, manic-depressive "fortune teller to the stars" Madame Lucille. As a result, Maz tried to be as normal as possible. Her plan goes haywire when her husband leaves her with two preteen daughters and her mother calls to announce her marriage to husband number six. Maz tries to settle back into domestic life after meeting a nice doctor, but will he get scared away when her ex and her wacky mother team up to kidnap one of her daughters? Funny characters and situations abound.

Strout, Elizabeth
Amy and Isabelle. 1998. Random House. ISBN 1568957289. 303p.

Isabelle shares a close relationship with her teenage daughter, Amy. When Amy falls in love with her high school math teacher, Isabelle becomes furious not only at the teacher, but at her daughter, for enjoying a life she herself has never known. As the scandal hits their gossipy small town, Isabelle finds herself at the center of judgment. An intense look at the bonds of love and jealousy between mothers and daughters.

Tan, Amy
The Bonesetter's Daughter. 2001. Putnam. ISBN 0399146431. 333p.

Tan looks at the relationship between a Chinese mother and her American-born daughter. Although the women have lived very different lives, their struggles to find their own identities are more alike then even they would have guessed. Tan is known for her evocative, well-drawn characters.

Thayer, Nancy
Family Secrets. 1993. Viking. ISBN 067084439X. 338p.

Diane worries about both her mother and her daughter in this story of three generations. Jean, Diane's mother, travels on a whirlwind European tour while Julia, Diane's teenage daughter, not sharing her mother's ambitions, fails in school. Diane always wanted to be different from her mom, whom she saw as just a housewife and mother. However, when the FBI starts investigating Jean's involvement in an antiwar movement in the 1940s, Diane realizes there is more to her mother's life than meets the eye. Meanwhile, Julia, grows desperate to escape from under Diane's thumb. A nicely drawn portrait of three different, yet similar, women.

Dissimilar Sisters

These stories of complete opposites show that you don't have to have the same personality to share the same bond.

Fleming, Anne Taylor
As If Love Were Enough: A Novel. 2006. Hyperion. ISBN 1401301053. 288p.

Clare, a writer, leads a fairly mundane life with no strings, which is how she likes it. Suddenly her long-estranged older sister, Louise, shows up at her doorstep. A nephew whom Clare never knew she had needs a kidney transplant, and Louise is hoping that Clare can write a publicity piece about him to help him move up on the transplant list. The novel shifts back to Clare and Louise's childhood, following them growing up with divorced Hollywood parents. The story of the sisters' estrangement unravels as the girls come of age in the 1960s.

Frankel, Valerie
Smart vs. Pretty. 2000. Avon. ISBN 0380805421. 304p.

Sisters Francesca and Amanda run the family coffee shop in Brooklyn Heights. When a chain coffee shop moves into the neighborhood, Francesca (the smart one) and Amanda (the pretty one) team up with a marketing student to revitalize the business. Frankel has a great knack for writing true to life characters.

Glass, Julia
I See You Everywhere. 2008. Pantheon. ISBN 0375422757. 304p.

Cautious and artistic Louisa and her restless, adventurous sister Clem are complete opposites—Louisa owns an art gallery in New York, while Clem is a wildlife specialist working with endangered species. This episodic novel follows the past 25 years of their lives, from joys to sorrows, culminating in a reunion at a family funeral. Competitive (they've been known to steal each other's boyfriends) and completely opposite, the sisters don't always understand each other but are always trying to do so.

Maxted, Anna
A Tale of Two Sisters. 2004. Dutton. ISBN 0525949739. 368p.

London sisters Lizbet and Cassie are different as night and day—Lizbet is scatterbrained but has a nice stable life, while glossy and high-powered Cassie leads a strained and stressful life. When Lizbet discovers she's unexpectedly pregnant, she and her boyfriend are overjoyed. Cassie, who's been longing for a child but is trapped in a loveless marriage, is less than happy for her sister. Similar to Maxted's other takes on chick lit, *A Tale of Two Sisters* has a bit of a harsh edge instead of the usual fun and fluff from the genre.

Robinson, Elisabeth
The True and Outstanding Adventures of the Hunt Sisters. 2004. Little, Brown. ISBN 0316735027. 272p.

Olivia Hunt, a Hollywood screenwriter whose career is dragging her down—she works with incompetent writers, egotistical directors and stars—is just about ready to throw in the towel. But when she finds out her younger sister Maddie has been diagnosed with leukemia, her life seems golden by comparison. Maddie, newly married, and determined to keep a cheerful face, needs her sister's help. At turns funny and sad, this story is never overly sentimental.

Upcher, Caroline
Grace and Favor. 2001. Kensington. ISBN 1575669048. 358p.

Grace and Pat were raised separately after their mother's suicide. Now a successful novelist living in the Hamptons, Grace finally meets her shy, London housewife sister (whom she dubs Favor, as in favored child) when the two are in their mid-40s. Finally, their unexplored past catches up with them. Good family secrets fiction with interesting characters.

Weiner, Jennifer
⇨ *In Her Shoes.* 2002. Atria. ISBN 0743418190. 432p.

Slightly frumpy and very dependable Rose allows her extremely pretty and very flighty sister, Maggie, to move in with her when Maggie loses yet another job. But Rose finally hits her limit when Maggie steals her shoes, her credit cards, and her boyfriend. The sisters are finally brought back together when the grandmother they never knew comes to seek them out. Weiner's novels are funny, smart, and touching, and this one doesn't disappoint in its portrayal of two very different sisters who think they don't need anyone discovering they truly need each other.

Nobody Told Me There'd Be Days Like These: Mommy Lit

These funny takes on motherhood tell it like it is in a humorous style.

Beaumont, Maria
37. 2008. Hyperion. ISBN 1401303196. 294p.

Fran was a successful voice-over artist before having kids and leaving the industry. Now that her two children are both in school, she's feeling unfulfilled and morose. The year she turns 37, she decides to sort everything out but is dreadfully unsuccessful. Egged on by a gossipy neighbor, she begins drinking heavily, at one point endangering her children. Things get worse as she suspects her husband of cheating on her, and she skips every audition she gets sent out on. When the school principal accuses her of being an unfit parent, she realizes it's really time to turn around and get her act together.

Center, Katherine
⇨ *The Bright Side of Disaster.* 2007. Random House. ISBN 1400066379. 256p.

When her boyfriend has a panic attack and leaves her the day before she gives birth, Jenny finds herself raising a baby alone. Her feisty mother comes to help, along with her stalwart best friend and a very cute neighbor who just keeps appearing whenever she needs his help. But what will Jenny do when her contrite boyfriend appears on her doorstep months later? A charming novel featuring realistic characters and laugh-out-loud situations.

Porter, Jane
Odd Mom Out. 2007. Warner 5-Spot. ISBN 0446699233. 432p.

Single mom Marta moves from New York back to Seattle, only to find she doesn't quite fit in with the local mommy set. She's camouflage and combat boots; they're pastels and high heels. This doesn't do much to help her nine-year-old daughter fit in, either. When Marta tries to fit in, she risks her sanity and her work life becomes threatened. What's an independent mom to do—is it impossible to have it all?

Scheibe, Amy
What Do You Do All Day? 2005. St. Martin's. ISBN 0312343035. 320p.

Jennifer, a former antiques expert for Christies, now spends her days raising five-year-old Georgia and baby Max. She's having a hard time preserving her identity and when her husband leaves for a three-month trip to Singapore, she decides to seek out other stay-at-home moms. This is *Sex and the City* crossed with *Parents Magazine.*

Weiner, Jennifer
Little Earthquakes. 2004. Atria. ISBN 0743470095. 432p.

Four unlikely friends bond over motherhood. While down-to-earth Becky deals with a tough mother-in-law; glamorous Ayinde worries that her basketball-star husband is having an affair; and Kelly tries to mother both her baby and her out-of-work husband. Lia, an outsider, observes the group of friends while hiding a tragic secret that makes her keep her distance. A realistic look at raising a baby while dealing with the rest of your life. If only life took naps...

Williams, Polly
The Yummy Mummy. 2007. Hyperion. ISBN 1401302319. 384p.

New mom Amy feels lost without her high-powered PR job at a prestigious British firm, yet she's not sure where to fit in now with a six-month-old in tow. She is torn between two groups of friends—the frumpier pals she made in her childbirth classes and the new friends she's dying to be a part of, the "Yummy Mummies." When new "yummy" friend Alice takes over Amy's life in a makeover she calls Project Amy, Amy's not really sure this is the life she belongs in, either.

Zigman, Laura
Piece of Work. 2006. Warner. ISBN 044657838X. 304p.

Julie's husband Peter loses his job, so she goes back to work as a celebrity publicist after three years as a stay-at-home mom. When she lands a difficult client, she quickly remembers that dealing with some adults is the same as dealing with toddlers. But worse than her work woes is the fact that she's jealous of her newly domestic husband and she misses her young son. A warm and witty look at the struggle between raising a family and having a career.

Pregnant Pauses

Before getting to the Mommy Lit, there's the step of Pregnant Lady Lit. Mostly fun and breezy, none of these will take you nine months to finish.

Bilston, Sarah
Bed Rest. 2006. Harper Collins. ISBN 0060889934. 224p.

Everything's been just fine for Quinn—she had has a great career as a lawyer and married a great husband and then had a great pregnancy—when all of a sudden she is put on bed rest for the last three months of her pregnancy. Her formerly busy, organized life comes to a screeching halt. When she makes friends with the neighbors, she finds a new purpose doing some pro bono work for the residents of the building next door. This element of the story lends some meat to the book, making it stand out from other chick lit fare.

Carbin, Debbie
Thanks for Nothing, Nick Maxwell. 2008. St. Martin's. ISBN 0312383681. 408p.

Rachel's life as a shallow, glamorous single gal comes to an abrupt halt when she discovers she's pregnant by a fling. Nausea and moodiness are enough to get her down, but what she really can't handle is the loss of her old lifestyle. When she meets a charming, respectful man, she realizes it's time to grow up and assume the responsibility of taking care of her new child. A sweet look at how having a baby changes everything.

Finnamore, Suzanne
The Zygote Chronicles. 2002. Grove. ISBN 0802117066. 144p.

This autobiographical novel is the journal of a first pregnancy. Funny and sharp, the narrator worries about her job, her body, and how her life will change. A short and sweet insight into impending motherhood.

Green, Jane
⇨ *Babyville.* 2003. Broadway. ISBN 0767912233. 432p.

Three friends cope with impending motherhood, wanted and unwanted. Julia struggles to conceive, but her boyfriend could care less. Maeve becomes unexpectedly (and scandalously) pregnant; and Samantha's postpartum depression takes a toll on her marriage. Green has a knack for endearing, realistic characters, and these three women provide great examples of her talent.

Green, Risa
Notes from the Underbelly. 2004. New American Library. ISBN 0451214161. 304p.

Lara, a counselor at a Bel-Air prep school, decides that working with kids is the best form of birth control, but her husband has other ideas. When they decide it's time to start a family, she finds herself completely unprepared for the changes she goes through, from those in her body to those in her life.

Although Lara and her friends may seem awfully shallow, this is still an entertaining read.

Holden, Wendy
The Wives of Bath. 2005. Plume. ISBN 0452285895. 292p.

Two very different expectant couples become friends when they attend a prenatal class in Bath, England. Alice, a lawyer, has married hippie environmentalist Jake after a one-night stand left them parents-to-be. Amanda, a celebrity journalist, is married to Hugo, a real estate agent, and they've left their high-powered careers in the city to move to the country life. Will these mismatched couples remain unlikely friends once the babies arrive? Holden's signature witty social commentary shines here.

Pearson, Patricia
Playing House. 2003. Avon Trade. ISBN 0060534370. 288p.

When Frannie discovers she's gotten pregnant accidentally, she flees home from New York to Toronto. Unfortunately, when she tries to return to the States, she discovers her visa has expired, leaving her jobless and forcing her to move into her brother's mansion as a housesitter while the family is on vacation. Alone, she must navigate nursing bras, morning sickness, and—oh yeah— tracking down her free-spirited globe-trotting boyfriend to share the news.

Webb, Kris, and Kathy Wilson
From Here to Maternity. 2004. Thomas Dunne. ISBN 0312327994. 288p.

Australian marketing executive Sydney discovers she's pregnant, and since her boyfriend just moved to San Francisco, it looks like she's going to be a single mom. That doesn't sit well with the party girl—and what about her career? When she and her friends decide to go into business creating baby books, it looks like she might just be able to handle a new life after all—until her boyfriend comes back into the picture. Smart and cute.

Wolf, Laura
Diary of a Mad Mom-to-Be. 2003. Delta. ISBN 0385336772. 321p.

Having managed to get her wedding out of the way, Amy, a control freak, now decides to embark on motherhood. She endures day-long morning sickness and immense lifestyle changes, including trying to adjust to a new career as a PR executive. Often over-the-top and sarcastic, this diary will appeal to those looking for the warts-and-all side of pregnancy.

What's the Matter with Kids These Days?

Think childbirth is tough? It's not easy being the mother of preteens and teenagers either.

Cleage, Pearl
   Babylon Sisters. 2005. Ballantine. ISBN 0345456092. 304p.

   Cat Sanderson has good life: a successful consulting business, a lovely home in Atlanta, and a wonderful teenage daughter, Phoebe. Things go sour, however, when Phoebe, in a fit of rebellion, contacts her mother's ex-boyfriends and demands DNA tests in order to find her real father, who Cat has been lying about for 17 years. Surprisingly enough, he has just reappeared in town. Can Cat manage to repair things with her daughter and make her understand?

Davey, Janet
   First Aid: A Novel. 2006. Back Bay Books. ISBN 9780316059978. 224p.

   After her divorce, Jo packs up her children to return to the London home of her grandparents. During the trip, while Jo is occupied with her two younger kids, teenage Ella jumps from the train and runs away. Unbelievably, Jo makes no attempt to find her, and once arriving in London lies to her family about Ella's absence. Ella, meanwhile, runs back to their old apartment, where she hides, visits her dad, and generally tries to work out what to do next.

Moriarty, Laura
   ⇨ *The Rest of Her Life.* 2007. Hyperion. ISBN 9781401302719. 320p.

   Leigh's teenage daughter Kara is responsible for killing a classmate in a car accident. As Leigh tries to cope with the aftermath and reach out to her daughter, Kara withdraws further and further. Leigh's own childhood was strained by a difficult relationship with her mother, so she's always tried to be part of her children's lives, but now Kara wants nothing more than to be left alone. Meanwhile, Leigh's son Justin feels ignored and unimportant. A smartly woven tale of a mother trying to connect to her teenage children in the wake of a tragedy.

Packer, Ann
   Songs without Words. 2007. Knopf. ISBN 9780375412813. 352p.

   Liz and Sarabeth, both in their 40s, have been friends since childhood. Liz is a down-to earth, responsible mother of two teenagers while Sarabeth is a free-spirited artist. When Liz's daughter attempts suicide, the bonds of their friendship are tested as Sarabeth withdraws just when Liz needs her most. Packer captures the angst of a depressed teen beautifully, with sensitivity and realism.

Seidel, Kathleen Gilles
   A Most Uncommon Degree of Popularity. 2006. St. Martin's. ISBN 0312333269.
      304p.

   Lydia is amazed at her daughter's popularity. A sixth-grader at a posh Washington, D.C., private school, Erin, a likeable girl, has close childhood friends who make up a popular clique. However, all of that changes when the girls hit middle school. When a new queen bee takes over and Erin's friends all join a vocal ensemble without her, she becomes sullen and difficult, and Lydia discovers her own social status has dropped as well, as the girls' mothers adopt the same pettiness as their teenage daughters.

Weiner, Jennifer
Certain Girls. 2008. Atria. ISBN 9780743294256. 384p.

Cannie, the heroine from Weiner's bestselling debut *Good in Bed* (2001), is now the mother of 13-year-old Joy. Joy, a smart girl, does poorly in school because she doesn't think it's cool to wear her hearing aids. She also battles daily with Cannie over her upcoming Bat Mitzvah—whereas Joy wants an all-out glam spectacle like her friends, including a Badgley Mishka dress, conservative Cannie wants a highly spiritual day. Their relationship gets tested further when Joy finally reads Cannie's semiautobiographical first novel, which leads her to believe she was an unwanted baby. Alternating chapters between the two characters paint a humorous portrait of a mom and teenage daughter lovingly at odds.

Willard, Katie
Raising Hope. 2005. Warner. ISBN 0446576875. 305p.

Preteen Hope is being raised by three very different women. Her aunt Ruth, a tough-talking waitress, is often at odds with her father's ex-girlfriend Sarah, a prim and wealthy lawyer. Put opinionated widow Aimee, Sarah's mother, into the mix, and you have a delightful cast of characters bound together by their affection for a young girl they've known since she was an infant.

Mothers-In-Law

The most clichéd of all clichés…these books will make you appreciate your own mother-in-law more and more—or they'll offer company if you have one who's just as bad!

Bartolomeo, Christina
Snowed In. 2004. St. Martin's. ISBN 0312320884. 373p.

After moving to Maine for her husband's job, Sophie finds herself with cabin fever, and her meddlesome mother-in-law Pepper is not helping things. Of course, Pepper doesn't think Sophie is good enough for her son and spares no opportunity to tell her so! When Sophie joins a neighborhood walking club and begins to meet new people, she heads towards the end of her marriage. That's just what Pepper really wants—but is that what Sophie really wants?

Dawson, Carol
The Mother-In-Law Diaries. 1999. Algonquin. ISBN 1565121279. 284p.

After her son gets married, Lulu comes to the bittersweet realization that she is now a mother-in-law. Having been married four times herself, she recounts the mothers-in-law of her past. Among them are Hazel the happy homemaker, always making Lulu feel second best; Filalia, a witch who practiced voodoo;

and Cassandra, who was interfering to the point of almost being abusive. Lulu is determined to figure out what kind of mother-in-law she will be. An insightful look at a woman's life reflected through her marriages and mother-in-laws.

Frankel, Valerie

I Take This Man. 2007. Avon. ISBN 0060785551. 320p.

In a different take on the story (usually it's the groom's mom who is painted as the bad guy), Penny's mom becomes the (almost) mother-in-law from hell. When Penny is jilted on the morning of her wedding, her mother Esther abducts her fiancé, Bram, and locks him away in her house for several weeks. In the meantime, Esther finds herself falling in love with Bram's father! Not exactly the best way to start out a relationship, indeed. Over-the-top but endearing just the same.

Green, Jane

⇨ *The Other Woman.* 2005. Viking. ISBN 0670034045. 400p.

When Ellie becomes engaged to Dan, the man of her dreams, his mother, Linda, becomes her worst nightmare. At first, Ellie hopes for a great relationship, as she grew up without her own mother. But the needy and controlling Linda knows exactly what buttons to push in order to get her way. When things with Linda go from bad to worse after Ellie and Dan have a baby, it puts Ellie's whole marriage in jeopardy. Green balances her trademark humor with serious issues in this novel.

Medwed, Mameve

Of Men and Their Mothers. 2008. William Morrow. ISBN 9780060831219. 304p.

When Maisie and Rex divorce, Maisie finds she's still not free of her mother-in-law Ina, who was a big factor in the breakup of the marriage. Ina is determined to have her say in how Maisie raises her teenage son, Tommy. Meanwhile, Tommy brings home a less-than-suitable girlfriend, prompting Maisie to contemplate what kind of mother-in-law she'd be someday. Quirky characters and gentle humor make this a good read.

Morsi, Pamela

By Summer's End. 2005. Mira. ISBN 0778321398. 378p.

After being diagnosed with cancer, Dawn is forced to move in with her in-laws, whom she hasn't spoken to since her husband's death 13 years earlier. Her mother-in-law, who considered Dawn to be socially inferior, never forgave Dawn for her son's accident. Despite the somber circumstances, Mori delivers the story with wit and insight into family relations.

Seidel, Kathleen Gilles

Keep Your Mouth Shut and Wear Beige. 2008. St. Martin's. ISBN 0312367740. 288p.

Divorced nurse Darcy finds herself the mother of the groom, an exciting prospect, since she truly likes the bride and her wealthy family. Unfortunately,

Darcy's ex-husband's girlfriend, Claudia, is determined to use the wedding as a way to promote her business and climb the social ladder. A Martha Stewart–wannabe, Claudia elbows her way in to all the planning and slowly threatens to take over. Can Darcy manage being a new mother-in-law and keep Claudia from ruining the day at the same time?

After He's Gone: Widow Lit

A recent trend in women's fiction, these titles explore life after love, for women of all ages. The following novels handle a sensitive subject without delving into sappiness.

Ahern, Cecelia
P.S. I Love You. 2004. Hyperion. ISBN 1401300901. 375p.

Holly discovers a year's worth of letters that her late husband Gerry left for her to read after his untimely death. Feeling that he is still close by keeping watch, she embarks on reclaiming her life. Holly's family and friends also play a large part in her growth. A sentimental story but not sappy.

Asher, Bridget
My Husband's Sweethearts. 2008. Delacorte. ISBN 038534189X. 288p.

Lucy is not quite a widow, but she's grieving all the same—after discovering her husband was cheating on her throughout their marriage, she leaves him, only to be called back home when he realizes he's dying of heart failure. Needing closure, she decides to call all the women in his little black book and have them come to say goodbye. Humorous yet poignant, this is an interesting look at a woman who gets time to make amends and get used to being a widow, before her husband's gone.

Frankel, Valerie
The Not So Perfect Man 2004. Avon. ISBN 978–0060536688. 368p.

Young widow Frieda has no interest in meeting another man, despite the protestations of her two sisters, who try to fix her up with anyone and everyone. Problem is, she can't help but compare each of the men to her late husband. That is, until she meets Sam, an out-of-work actor who is totally wrong for her and her young son, at least according to everyone else.

King, Cassandra
Queen of Broken Hearts. 2007. Hyperion. ISBN 978–1401301774. 400p.

Since the death of her husband in a mysterious hunting accident, 50-something divorce coach Clare has thrown herself into her work. She finds it hard to be off the clock, however, and also throws herself into her friends' lives while ignoring her own needs. She watches her patients and friends go forward while she is stuck in the past, refusing to let a new man into her life, until two different men start competing for her attention.

Lissner, Caren

Starting from Square Two. 2004. Red Dress Ink. ISBN 978–0373250523. 304p.

Gert's been a widow for a year and a half, and her two best friends think it's time she started dating again. Reluctantly, Gert follows them out on the town and meets Tom, a sweet guy who is completely different from her husband. But is Gert ready to start a new life, or does she still need time to come into her own?

Samson, Lisa

The Living End. 2003. Waterbrook Press. ISBN 1578565979. 306p.

When Pearly's husband Joey dies from a stroke after 35 years of marriage, she is devastated. Thinking she could never live without him, she contemplates suicide—but then finds a tattered note in one of his jacket pockets. Titled "While I Live, I Want To . . . ," she realizes it's a list of things he always wanted to do, but never had the chance. She decides to fulfill his wish list herself, including getting a tattoo and visiting the pyramids. Along the way she meets many quirky characters who convince her that life is worth living, even without her beloved husband.

Sheepshanks, Mary

Picking Up the Pieces. 1997. St. Martin's. ISBN 031219997X. 290p.

Recently widowed, Kate finds herself living in a sprawling English manor with her mother-in-law, her daughter, and her grandchildren. Tired of being the housekeeper and caretaker, she decides to pursue her dream of opening a craft shop but meets all kinds of obstacles along the way, from family to financial. A lovely, humorous family tale showcasing a widow about to embark on a new life.

Winston, Lolly

⇨ *Good Grief.* 2004. Warner. ISBN 978–0446533041. 352p.

When 36-year-old Sophie Stanton goes from newlywed to widow in just three short years of marriage, she learns that instead of the 5 stages of grief, there are 14: Denial, Oreos, Anger, Bargaining, Depression, Ashes, Lust, Waitressing, Mentoring, Dating, Baking, Acceptance, Goodwill, and Thanksgiving. After a brief breakdown when she loses her job for showing up in her robe and bunny slippers, Sophie sells her house and moves to Oregon to find herself and lose her grief.

Here Comes the Bride

Like the best gossip, tales of Bridezillas, crazy friends, obnoxious wedding planners, and the general feeling of "what can go wrong, will go wrong" somehow make us feel better about our own lives.

Alan, Theresa
Getting Married. 2007. Kensington. ISBN 0758209967. 320p.

Eva, a successful management consultant, finds her life turned upside down when she meets a man online, moves in with him, and impulsively accepts his marriage proposal. Will isn't the problem—he's charming and sweet—what stresses her is planning a perfect wedding, and trying to keep up with her career, and trying to run a household for two, and trying to overcome her fear of commitment, and her jealousy over Will's ex-wife...which all leads her to succumb to a drug addiction. Definitely not your standard bridal fare, but a serious subject is treated with finesse and light humor.

Finnamore, Suzanne
Otherwise Engaged. 1999. Knopf. ISBN 0375406522. 209p.

San Francisco ad-writer Eve chronicles her 12-month engagement to her boyfriend Michael in this witty novel. She finds herself wondering if she can manage all the pressure and the changes, as well as a sudden fear of commitment. Does she really want to get married, or is she just going along with what's expected of her?

Kendrick, Beth
Nearlyweds. 2006. Downtown Press. ISBN 0743499603. 352p.

A different take on typical bridal chick lit, this is the story of three women who discover that their marriage paperwork was never filed—so they aren't really married. Would they do it again or is this the perfect time to run out? Casey is fed up with her immature husband; Stella discovers a relationship-altering secret; and Erin has had it with her mother-in-law. Clever and well-written.

Kinsella, Sophie
⇨ *Shopaholic Ties the Knot.* 2003. Delta. ISBN 0385336179. 327p.

Becky Bloomwood, star of *Confessions of a Shopaholic* (2001) and *Shopaholic Takes Manhattan* (2002), is finally getting married—twice even? Seems she can't decide whether it's to be at the Plaza in New York City or in her parent's backyard in England...so she agrees to both on the same day. She certainly wants to please her mum and have a pretty garden wedding with the family, but it's hard for a shopaholic to resist the lure of the Plaza. Wacky Becky will have you shaking your head, mostly out of laughter.

Lyles, Whitney
Here Comes the Bride. 2006. Berkley. ISBN 0425211304. 304p.

Cate is finally a bride after being a bridesmaid four times in one year (in the prequel to this book, *Always the Bridesmaid*). Things don't go smoothly, however, when her fiancé's ex-girlfriend won't stay out of the picture, her mom won't stay out of the wedding plans, and moving in together is not quite the picture of domestic bliss she envisioned. Charming and cute.

Senate, Melissa
Whose Wedding is it Anyway? 2004. Red Dress Ink. ISBN 0373250770. 304p.

At first, Eloise is thrilled that working at *Wow Weddings* magazine means she'll get the whole shebang paid for and featured in an upcoming issue. But when her conniving boss starts to take over every last detail (including choosing a feathery yellow bridal gown), she's not sure how her dream wedding became such a nightmare. It's enough to make a girl start to wonder if she even wants to get married at all . . .

Wolf, Laura
Diary of a Mad Bride. 2002. Delta. ISBN 0385335830. 294p.

The secret to control-freak Amy's success has always been lists, so it's no surprise that she ends up with 70 items on her wedding to-do list. Too bad the lists don't actually help her make up her mind. She's certain she won't change her name but then changes her mind. Heck, she always thought she'd never be interested in getting married! Comic and fast-paced, this is one heck of a Bridezilla novel.

There Goes the Bride

Tales of women coping after divorce. From young brides to seasoned wives, here are tales of women emerging triumphant from difficult situations.

Berg, Elizabeth
Open House. 2000. Random House. ISBN 0375501002. 201p.

Samantha's husband finally walks out after 20 years of a crumbling marriage, leaving her with no job, a house to pay for, and a preteen son. After a $12,000 wacky spending spree, she realizes it's time to get serious if she wants to keep the house and her sanity. To help with the mortgage, she decides to open her house to roomers. The various people she meets and becomes friends with boost her self confidence; and she discovers there really is life after divorce. A wonderful story of self discovery.

Dunn, Jancee
Don't You Forget About Me. 2008. Villard. ISBN 034550190X. 276p.

New Yorker Lillian is a senior citizen trapped in a 30-something's body. She's a homebody, enjoys old movies and TV shows, and even works as the producer of a talk show aimed at the over 70 crowd. Unfortunately, her husband is not thrilled with this lifestyle and stuns her by telling her he wants a divorce. Adrift, Lillian moves in with her parents, back to her girlhood room—a shrine to the late 1980s. In anticipation of her high school reunion, Lillian not only reconnects with her old girlfriends and wonders if she might get another shot with her high school sweetheart.

Heller, Jane
An Ex to Grind. 2005. Morrow. ISBN 0060599251. 384p.

Manhattan banker Melanie discovers that she is responsible for a large alimony settlement to keep her ex-husband Dan in the lifestyle he's grown accustomed to. So, she enlists a matchmaker to bring her husband up to snuff and find him a new love. The plan backfires, however, when it works too well, and Melanie finds the new and improved Dan a lot better than the old one.

Matthews, Carole
For Better, For Worse. 2002. Avon. ISBN 0380820447. 242p.

Newly divorced, Josie's self-esteem needs a shot in the arm. On a transatlantic flight, she begins to flirt with Matt, the cute journalist sitting next to her, and they make plans to meet up in New York City for some sightseeing. Zaniness ensues when they miss their appointed meeting time, Josie's ex decides to cross the pond to try and win her back, and Matt desperately tries to track Josie down. A fun chick lit take on how divorce can be a great boost you didn't know you needed.

Moore, Jane
⇨ *Fourplay.* 2002. Broadway. ISBN 0767913000. 384p.

When her cheating husband leaves, interior designer Jo worries that she is now part of the "undateable" caste—30-somethings with small kids. She takes a leap of faith back into the dating world. The title refers to four men she begins to juggle, none of them very desirable—a sleaze who is cheating on his wife, one of her clients, her brother's best friend, and lo and behold, her ex. A fast-paced and funny tale.

Royal, Anastasia
Undoing I Do. 2007. Thomas Dunne. ISBN 0312369654. 426p.

Claire and Tobin had a seemingly perfect life—a storybook wedding, two wonderful children, satisfying careers, and a lovely home. Then one day, Tobin unexpectedly walks out, leaving Claire stunned. She realizes her life as an artist is not going to pay the bills but is so devastated by Tobin's rejection that she doesn't quite know how to care for herself and her children without him. Can she pull herself up and out in order to put her life back together again?

Satran, Pamela Redmond
The Man I Should Have Married. 2003. Downtown Press. ISBN 0743463544. 287p.

When her husband of 10 years leaves her, Kennedy reaches for the independence she never had. She begins to revisit her New York City haunts and meets up with hunky bartender Declan, a former flame. Kennedy manages to delicately balance a rekindled romance and a variety of life changes with the responsibility of caring for her two daughters, with deft humor.

Wolff, Isabel
Rescuing Rose. 2004. Red Dress Ink. ISBN 0373250487. 443p.

Rose, a London advice columnist, is in need of advice herself when she gets divorced after only seven months of marriage. She buys a house and takes on a roommate, Theo, whom she begins to have feelings for. But what happens when her ex decides he wants to get back together?

Unhappy in Their Own Way

Tolstoy said it best—"Happy families are all alike; every unhappy family is unhappy in its own way" (*Anna Karenina*).

Battle, Lois
Bed & Breakfast. 1997. Penguin. ISBN 0140259112. 372p.

Three daughters return home for Christmas and unlock family secrets. A decade of blame and misunderstandings has kept estranged Cam, the eldest, alone and away from her family, worrying about her career and her boyfriend. Middle sister Lila has enough problems in her own family, with an anorexic daughter and a boring husband. Evie, the youngest, spills her secrets in her newspaper column. A delicate portrait of a family at odds.

Cadwalladr, Carol
Family Tree. 2005. Dutton. ISBN 0525948422. 416p.

Rebecca Monroe, an academic and a child of 1970s Britain, studies her own upbringing through the pop culture of the period. Her scientist husband explains everything through genetics and uses Rebecca's dysfunctional and unhappy family as a genetic study of mental illness. But can science alone explain her family history or her mother's depression and suicide? When Rebecca discovers she's pregnant and investigates the past, she begins to doubt her husband's certainty that genes determine our destinies.

Gamble, Terry
The Good Family: A Novel. 2005. Morrow. ISBN 0060737948. 318p.

When her mother has a stroke, Maddie reluctantly returns home to her family's vacation spot on Lake Michigan. Maddie's got enough of her own troubles, as a recovering alcoholic still struggling to get over the death of her infant daughter. She certainly doesn't need to revisit the ghosts of the past gathered back home, including dysfunctional cousins, a wild sister, and assorted family secrets. Or does she?

Haigh, Jennifer
The Condition. 2008. HarperCollins. ISBN 0060755784. 390p.

Young Gwen McKotch is diagnosed with Turner's Syndrome, a genetic disease that leaves her with infertility, stunted growth, and possible health problems. Her parents never quite come to terms with the illness and the subsequent tension propels their already shaky marriage to a bitter divorce. Meanwhile, Gwen's two brothers are left to flounder as they grow up. When a family reunion on Cape Cod brings them back together after years of infighting, will the bond of family be enough to reconnect their relationships?

Lamott, Anne

Blue Shoe. 2002. Riverhead Books. ISBN 1573222267. 304p.

When Mattie leaves her husband and moves in with her increasingly ailing mother, she uncovers a host of family secrets. Mattie has her own problems, since she's still sleeping with her ex, who has just moved in with his girlfriend and their new baby. She also finds herself drawn to a friend's husband. Are these the effects of growing up with an adulterous father and an intimidating mother?

Moriarty, Laura

⇨ *The Center of Everything.* 2003. Hyperion. ISBN 1401300316. 291p.

A sensitive and moving portrait of a precocious girl, Evelyn, and her single mom, living just shy of real poverty in 1980s-era Kansas. Evelyn is bright and could go far, were it not for her irresponsible mother and bible-thumping grandmother. Evelyn's mom, already disowned by her father, gets pregnant by her married boss and can't see past her own troubles to care for Evelyn. Moriarty's gift for true-to-life characters and scenes will break your heart and make you cheer for the characters to do well.

Tucker, Lisa

Once Upon a Day: A Novel. 2006. Atria. ISBN 0743492773. 342p.

After a nervous breakdown caused by a vicious attack on his wife, Charles O'Brien shelters his children in an isolated New Mexico estate without access to computers, television, or any form of communication with the outside world. When he becomes seriously ill, his 23-year-old daughter Dorothea escapes to search for her runaway older brother. This lyrical novel features a sympathetic cast of characters, a portrait of a family haunted by fate, loss, and forgiveness.

Ward, Amanda Eyre

How to Be Lost. 2004. MacAdam Cage. ISBN 1931561729. 290p.

On the day that Caroline her sisters decide to run away from home, the youngest girl goes missing. The focus here is not the missing girl, but the unstable family as a whole. An abusive, alcoholic father and a mother in the throes of depression drive the two remaining girls into their own dysfunctional adulthoods. Caroline can't commit to anything and doesn't want to grow up; and repressed Madeline has distanced herself from everyone and everything. When Caroline convinces herself that a magazine photo of a woman is her long-lost sister, she revisits the ghosts from the past.

Putting the Fun in Dysfunctional

These are stories about quirky families, who are not necessarily unhappy, but definitely dysfunctional.

Allen, Sarah Addison
The Sugar Queen. 2008. Bantam Dell. ISBN 0553805495. 288p.

Quiet, quirky Josey prefers being a homebody, even though her mother, hiding from an unfulfilled past, treats her like dirt most of the time. That's OK with Josey though: she doesn't expect much else from her mother and is fine retreating to her room where she can gorge herself on her hidden cache of sweet treats. When outspoken wild child Della Lee appears, hiding out in Josey's closet, she convinces Josey to stand up for herself, seek the truth about her family, and finally make a move on the hunky mailman. Charming and surprising.

Andrews, Mary Kay
Savannah Blues. 2002. HarperCollins. ISBN 006019958X. 404p.

Eloise "Weezie" Foley is an antiques trader who lives in the carriage house behind the beautiful historic house she and her ex-husband once shared. He now shares that house with his sexy new fiancée—or at least he did, until said Weezie finds the woman dead. Weezie's gay ex-priest uncle acts as her legal counsel while her alcoholic mother and loopy best friend round out the mix of quirky characters. Great fun.

De Los Santos, Marisa
Love Walked In. 2005. Dutton. ISBN 0525949178. 320p.

Cornelia becomes part of a dysfunctional family when she falls for handsome Martin. Martin seems like an old-time movie star and things are pretty perfect until one day he shows up at Cornelia's café with the secret he's been hiding—his 10-year-old daughter, Claire. Claire's mother has had a mental breakdown and left Claire to fend for herself. Although Cornelia never thought she had it in her to be a parent or role model, she finds herself relishing the role of mom, even as her relationship with Martin loses its luster.

Jackson, Joshilyn
Between, Georgia. 2006. Warner. ISBN 0446524425. 304p.

Nonny has not one, but two dysfunctional families, and now she's stuck in a family feud that began the night she was born. Her biological family, the Crabtrees, are the poor lawless outcasts of their rural Georgia town; while her adopted family, the Fretts, are the upper-crust, can-do-no-wrong type. Her adopted mother is blind and deaf; her rocker husband is always half out the door; and her biological grandmother sets her Dobermans on anyone she doesn't like. Funny and poignant, this is a story of two polar opposite families with more in common than they think.

Pedersen, Laura
Beginners Luck. 2003. Ballantine. ISBN 0345458303. 368p.

Bored with school, bored with life, Hallie feels lost in her large family. When mom and dad announce the impending arrival of sibling number eight, she runs away (just down the block) to become a groundskeeper of sorts for the eccentric Stockton family. Matriarch Olivia is a free-spirited throwback from the 1960s, spouting politics and feminism, while taking care of her Alzheimer's-stricken husband. Son Bertie and his boyfriend Gil are cultured foodies who delight in introducing Hallie to fine cinema and antiques. And then there's the alcoholic chimpanzee . . .

Schwartz, Lynne Sharon
In the Family Way: An Urban Comedy. 1999. William Morrow. ISBN 0688170714. 325p.

Bea and her ex-husband Roy live in an apartment building on the Upper West Side, surrounded by their extended family. Bea's randy widowed mother Anna owns the building; Roy's second wife is now the lesbian lover of Bea's sister; and Bea's Russian lover is the building's super—and that's only the tenants of the first few apartments. Their kids and various exes live there, too. It doesn't get much quirkier than this.

Toews, Miriam
The Flying Troutmans: A Novel. 2008. Counterpoint. ISBN 1582434395. 224p.

The Troutman clan has troubles. Min is bedridden by mental illness and her teenage son has been expelled from school, so her preteen daughter Thebes makes a frantic phone call to Min's sister Hattie. Hattie, living in Paris, has just been dumped by her moochy boyfriend, so she rushes back to Manitoba, Canada, to try and save her sister's family from falling apart. When Min is hospitalized after attempting suicide, Hattie takes the kids on a road trip to America to find the children's long-absent father. Biting wit and quirky characters abound.

West, Michael Lee
⇨ *Mermaids in the Basement.* 2008. HarperCollins. ISBN 0060184051. 304p.

Screenwriter Renata comes from a true Southern family, complete with a formidable grand-dame grandmother. Mourning the death of her mother, Renata escapes to her grandmother's cottage, but instead of finding rest and relaxation, she finds more stress, thanks to her family. Eventually, she discovers that her parents led secret lives to which she was never privy, until now: grandmother Honora and pals have decided it's time to let all of the skeletons out of the family closets. And to top matters off, when her father's new fiancée is found unconscious in the pool at their engagement party, Renata becomes the prime suspect. Even Daddy's not sure whether Renata's guilty of pushing the deranged starlet in!

I Get By with a Little Help...

Who doesn't rely on their girlfriends? You'll wish you were part of these circles.

Graham, Laurie
The Future Homemakers of America. 2002. Warner. ISBN 0446679364. 440p.

Five wives of air force pilots meet in England at the end of World War II, and this novel follows their friendship over 40 years. They encounter marital strife, money woes, bouts of illness, but their one constant is a strong bond of friendship. Nicely drawn characters and humor make this a good choice in the female friendship category.

Kelly, Cathy
Best of Friends. 2005. Downtown Press. ISBN 0743490258. 528p.

Four Irish best friends band together in this charming novel. Divorced Lizzie worries about being alone; TV star Abby frets about growing older; beauty salon owner Sally is always too busy; and Erin is obsessed with family secrets. When Sally is diagnosed with breast cancer, the women realize their problems are insignificant and Lizzie, Abby, and Erin rally together to support Sally.

King, Cassandra
Same Sweet Girls. 2005. Hyperion. ISBN 1401300383. 416p.

Six college friends who have met up twice a year for 30 years are preparing for a trip to Alabama when one of them becomes terminally ill, testing the strength of their bond. Nearing 50, they realize they are not really the "Same Sweet Girls" they always thought they'd stay. Julia is now the discontented first lady of Alabama, Lanier has had a marriage-ending affair, and Corrine battles depression. Byrd, Astor, and Rosanelle round out the gang.

Landvik, Lorna
⇨ *Angry Housewives Eating Bon Bons.* 2003. Ballantine. ISBN 0345438825. 336p.

Five housewives in small-town Minnesota meet in the turbulent late 1960s and form a book club. There's socially and politically active Slip; young widow Kari; meek and shy Merit; sexy and audacious Audrey; and transplanted Southerner Faith, who's not too thrilled with the Minnesotan tundra. The book follows the women to the present day, as they form close ties and act as sounding boards, partners in crime, and rescuers for one another.

Mapson, Jo-An
Bad Girl Creek. 2001. Simon & Schuster. ISBN 0743202562. 381p.

Beryl, Nance, Phoebe, and Ness come together to take over Phoebe's newly inherited flower farm. As they work to overcome the farm's problems, they support each other to defeat their personal problems. Phoebe is wheelchair bound due to congenital heart problems; Ness is out of work and fears she may have a serious illness; Nance is down-on-her-luck and lonely; and ex-convict Beryl has just been evicted from her home. These women, from such different backgrounds and experiences, form a tight bond and realize that they can overcome anything as long as they have their friends along for the ride.

Radish, Kris

Annie Freeman's Fabulous Traveling Funeral. 2006. Bantam. ISBN 0553382640. 352p.

When Annie dies of ovarian cancer, she leaves a package for her best friend, Katherine. The package contains her ashes (enclosed in red high-top sneakers) and instructions to gather her four best friends from across the country for a road trip, to scatter her ashes in meaningful places. Secrets about the women are revealed as they get to know one another better on the trip. A story about friendship and self-discovery.

Thayer, Nancy

Hot Flash Club. **Hot Flash Club Series.** 2003. Ballantine. ISBN 0345468627. 320p.

Four women meet at a retirement party and discover they have lots in common, despite their different backgrounds. Widowed artist Faye, career woman Alice, beautiful and brainy Marilyn, and New Age-y Shirley make it through menopause with a sense of humor, solving each other's problems—ranging from dealing with adult children to philandering husbands.

Trollope, Joanna

Friday Nights. 2008. Bloomsbury. ISBN 9781596914070. 336p.

Retired Eleanor invites two single young moms, Paula and Lindsay, over to her house for coffee one evening, starting a Friday night tradition. Soon the circle widens to include other women from the neighborhood. When Paula finds a new boyfriend, who insinuates himself into their circle, it upsets the balance and threatens to ruin lives.

Wells, Rebecca

Divine Secrets of the Ya-Ya Sisterhood. 1996. HarperCollins. ISBN 0060173289. 368p.

True, this is a story of a dysfunctional mother–daughter relationship. It's also a novel about finding yourself as you discover secrets about your past. But what really stands out in this story is the grand friendship of the Ya-Ya Sisterhood, four childhood best friends who grow up to be amazing, if crazy, women. Ringleader Vivi is glamorous and fearless. Teensy is the spunky, more common sense one. Caro is strong and noble, while Necie rounds out the group as the pious, conservative one. Follow their wild adventures as girls in the 1940s through their sobering, tough times as mothers and wives, and you'll laugh and cry along the way.

Of a Certain Age

These novels feature seasoned, "mature" women—who don't always act their age!

Cohen, Paula Marantz
⇨ *Jane Austen in Boca.* 2002. St. Martin's. ISBN 0312290888. 288p.

A loose adaptation of *Pride and Prejudice,* updated and set in a Florida retirement village. May is a gentle woman in her 70s; Lila is a merry widow in search of a rich husband; and Flo is a sassy retired librarian. When men enter the picture, you can bet there will be discord among the friends. Social commentary abounds in this fun look at the modern retirement scene.

Flagg, Fannie
Fried Green Tomatoes at the Whistle Stop Café. 1987. Random House. ISBN 039456152X. 403p.

Ninny Threadgoode, a spry 86 years old, recounts her adventures in 1930s–era Alabama to Evelyn, a visitor at Ninny's nursing home. The Whistle Stop Café, run by two outspoken women ahead of their time, forms the central setting for Ninny's funny and heartwarming stories of courage, love, and friendship.

Medlicott, Joan
The Ladies of Covington Send Their Love. **Ladies of Covington Series.** 2000. St. Martin's. ISBN 031225329X. 326p.

In the first novel of the series, we meet Grace, Hannah, and Amelia, three friends living in a retirement boarding house near Philadelphia. When Amelia inherits a crumbling farmhouse in Covington, North Carolina, the women pack up and set off for a new chapter in their lives. A charming tale of independent, thriving older women.

Ross, Ann B.
Miss Julia Speaks Her Mind. **Miss Julia Series.** 1999. William Morrow. ISBN 0786222557. 273p.

Recently widowed after 44 years of marriage to a minister, proper Miss Julia discovers that her late husband left her not only his estate—but a surprise nine-year-old son as well. When the boy's mother skips town, feisty, opinionated Julia discovers she has the mettle to take charge of events and turn her idle life into an eventful one.

Shaffer, Louise
The Three Miss Margarets. 2003. Random House. ISBN 037550852X. 324p.

Three Margarets—better known as Li'l Bit, Maggie, and Peggy—share a tight friendship and dark secrets. As upstanding Georgia ladies, they'd never admit to involvement in any scandal—they said all that was needed to be said long ago. When an old murder case comes back to haunt them, they must stand united to see the truth come out. Each Miss Margaret has her own complex and independent personality, lending richness to the story.

Willett, Marcia
The Children's Hour. 2004. Thomas Dunne Books. ISBN 0312327773. 367p.

Nest and Mina, sisters in their 70s living on the English coast, are worried when their ailing older sister Georgie comes to live with them. Georgie is on the brink of Alzheimer's and threatens to spill long-dormant family secrets. Complex characters and a riveting family saga from British author Willett.

Yglesias, Helen
The Girls. 1999. Delphinium. ISBN 188328516X. 213p.

Four sisters cope with growing old gracefully. Jenny, Flora, Naomi, and Eva, range in age from 80 to 95 and have come together to live in Florida and take care of one another. Jenny, the youngest, realizes that even in old age she has not overcome jealousies and hurt feelings from childhood. Flora, a geriatric sexpot, still bickers with her sisters as though they were teenagers. Naomi struggles with cancer, and Eva slowly fades. A sumptuous character study.

With Friends Like These...

Ah, the cattiest of females. What do you do when your friends let you down?

De Los Santos, Marisa
Belong to Me. 2008. Morrow. ISBN 0061240273. 400p.

Cornelia and Teo, best friends since childhood and now happily married, move to the suburbs to start a family. When Cornelia meets the beguiling and mysterious free spirit Lake, the two women become fast friends. Unfortunately, Lake has an ulterior motive and is keeping a big secret from her new friend.

Giffin, Emily
Something Borrowed. 2004. St. Martin's. ISBN 031232118X. 336p.

Shy Rachel falls in love with her best friend Darcy's fiancé, Dex. Rachel and Dex knew each other first, but bossy Darcy swooped in and took him over. Now, regretting the engagement and finding himself as drawn to Rachel as she is to him, they embark on an affair. In a twist, since Darcy is actually shallow and mean, Rachel becomes the sympathetic character even though she's the Other Woman.

Hannah, Kristin
Firefly Lane. 2008. St. Martin's. ISBN 9780312364083. 496p.

Since the mid-1970s Tully and Kate have been inseparable best friends. Drama queen Tully found stability with shy Kate's loving family, and they thought they'd be friends forever. The women grow up, move into careers, and fall in love; Kate, however, falls in love with Tully's ex-boyfriend. Fast-forward 30 years and Tully, a successful television journalist betrays stay-at-home mom Kate on live television when she accuses her of being a bad mother. Will the power of their friendship recover? A tear-jerker for sure.

Heller, Jane
Best Enemies. 2004. St. Martin's. ISBN 0312288492. 336p.

Since high school, Amy has always played second fiddle to her best friend, Tara. When Amy catches her fiancé and Tara together, she cuts them both out of her life. Tara marries the lout, and Amy becomes a top PR woman. When Tara writes a book about her perfect lifestyle—a total lie, by the way—Amy is, naturally, assigned to promote it. Hilarity ensues.

Keyes, Marian
The Other Side of the Story. 2004. Morrow. ISBN 0060520515. 528p.

Three women—Gemma, Jojo, and Lily—are all connected. Gemma and Lily were best friends until Lily stole Gemma's man. Lily is an author and Jojo is her London agent. When Gemma writes hysterical emails about her parent's breakup that find their way to Jojo, Jojo wants to turn them into a book, much to the jealous dismay of Lily, who is finding that life with Gemma's ex is not at all what she expected.

Niederhoffer, Galt
The Romantics. 2008. St. Martin's. ISBN 0312373376. 277p.

Nine college pals reunite at a wedding, only to have their already tenuous friendships put to the test. Lila and Tom are getting married, but Laura is not sure she wants to attend—she was Tom's ex-girlfriend and sure that he was The One. She certainly shouldn't be the maid of honor. Add three other couples to the mix, all in various stages of fighting, and it's a recipe for disaster. When Tom goes missing the night before the wedding, Laura is sure that he's got cold feet and will come back to her, since after all, he's only marrying the shallow Lila for her money. Or is he?

Stewart, Leah
⇨ *The Myth of You & Me.* 2005. Shaye Areheart Books. ISBN 1400098068. 288p.

Cameron and Sonia were best friends from junior high to post-college, until they had a huge falling out. After not speaking for 10 years, Sonia sends Cameron a letter announcing her engagement, prompting Cameron to track her down and unravel a mystery. A deftly told tale of young women and friendship.

We're All the Same After All: Multicultural Reads

African American

Here's a variety of good reads featuring African American women dealing with the same sorts of issues any woman could face.

Bandele, Asha
Daughter: A Novel. 2003. Scribner. ISBN 0743211847. 266p.
Miriam's world is rocked when her college-age daughter is killed by a white police officer in a case of mistaken identity. Having already lost her husband to police violence, she now loses her daughter just as they were trying to connect. Miriam reflects on what might have been and the tenuous bond between mothers and daughters.

Briscoe, Connie
P.G. County. 2002. Doubleday. ISBN 0385501617. 336p.
Barbara and Bradford Bentley reside in one of the country's most affluent African American neighborhoods, Prince George's County, Maryland. In this soapy novel, Barbara reigns over a group of neighbors including the adulteress Jolene, white hippie Candice, and hairdresser Pearl. When a runaway teenager, looking for her unknown father, enters the scene, drama ensues. Followed by *Can't Get Enough* (2006).

Campbell, Bebe Moore
⇨ *Singing in the Comeback Choir.* 1998. Putnam. ISBN 0399142983. 372p.
No one can deny that Maxine, the executive producer for a successful TV talk show, has a stressful life. Her Hollywood career ebbs and flows with the ratings, her husband has cheated on her, and she worries about her grandmother, Lindy, a woman who refuses to leave her dangerous Philadelphia neighborhood. Maxine was grateful for her grandmother's role in her upbringing, but was also happy to escape the rough neighborhood. When Lindy has a small stroke, Maxine must leave Los Angeles to assist her. A wonderful story of a grandmother and granddaughter who both want the best for each other.

Griffin, Bettye
Nothing But Trouble. 2006. Dafina. ISBN 9780758207395. 304p.
Three best friends find their relationships tested when one of their sisters enters the picture. Widowed Dana is on the verge of bankruptcy, Norelle desperately longs for a baby, and Cecile is already feeling the pinch raising a stepfamily when she discovers she's pregnant again. When Cecile's sexy younger sister Micheline moves to town and starts hitting on the friends' men, Cecile needs to decide between her sister and her friends.

McFadden, Bernice
Nowhere Is a Place. 2006. Dutton. ISBN 9780525948759. 416p.

In this multigenerational saga, 38-year-old Sherry, a wanderer, is always looking for a place to belong. She sets off with her estranged mother, Dumpling, on a days-long road trip to a family reunion in Georgia. Along the way, Sherry gets Dumpling to tell her family stories, from slavery to the present, and uncovers family secrets. This leads the women to discover who they really are and what kind of relationship they need to have.

Roby, Kimberla Lawson
A Taste of Reality. 2003. William Morrow. ISBN 0060505656. 292p.

Anise has a great life—an MBA, a successful husband, a dream home. But underneath the surface, she's unhappy—her company won't give her the projects she wants (because she's black and female) and she discovers her husband is cheating on her with a white woman. She decides she's had enough and musters up the courage to fight back. An excellent look at racial issues and the triumph of a strong woman.

Skerrett, Joanne
Sugar vs. Spice. 2006. Kensington Strapless. ISBN 9780758211538. 322p.

Tari is a newspaper journalist by day and an aspiring jazz singer by night. Her older sister Melinda, a wife, mother, and career woman, would like to see Tari follow in her more sensible footsteps, but Tari enjoys her carefree life. When Tari discovers she has breast cancer, she decides to conceal her illness from her coworkers and fellow musicians, with disastrous results. Luckily her family rallies around her when she needs them most.

Williams, Tia
The Accidental Diva. 2004. Putnam. ISBN 0399152016. 245p.

Uptown girl meets downtown boy. Billie Burke is the beauty editor of a leading national magazine. She loves her glamorous, upscale life in New York City and is on the brink of a promotion when she meets Jay, a performance artist with a shady past. Can their worlds ever combine, or are they just too different to make it work? A fun insider look at the beauty industry as well as a serious look at how your past can make you or break you.

Asian American

Here's a variety of good reads featuring Asian American women dealing with the same sorts of issues any woman could face.

Hwang, Caroline
In Full Bloom. 2003. Dutton. ISBN 0525947116. 304p.

Ginger Lee, a young assistant at a fashion magazine, is fine with her life the way it is. Her mother, however, is not and shows up on Ginger's Manhattan doorstep determined to find a nice Korean husband for her daughter. Ginger, whose interest in her Korean heritage is limited to food, is appalled by this notion, but Mom helps pay the bills, so what's a girl to do? Slowly Ginger learns to grow up and take control of her life while keeping her family happy.

Jen, Gish

The Love Wife: A Novel. 2004. Knopf. ISBN 1400042135. 400p.

Lan Lin arrives from China to work as a nanny for her distant cousin's family. The Wong family consists of second-generation Carnegie, his wife Blondie, their two adopted daughters and their son. Carnegie's mother, Mama Wong, never wanted him to marry the white Blondie, even going so far as to offer her a million dollars to stay away from her son. When Lan shows up, sent by Mama, Blondie suspects ulterior motives as the children cling to her and her husband gains a newfound interest in his Chinese heritage.

Keltner, Kim Wong

The Dim Sum of All Things. 2003. Avon Trade. ISBN 0060560754. 344p.

Third-generation Chinese American Lindsey Owyang has very little in common with her heritage. She lives with her grandmother, Pau Pau, who keeps a traditional way of life (including playing major mahjong tournaments). When the two women travel from San Francisco to China to visit long-lost family, Lindsey gains a new appreciation for her background and history as she is immersed in Chinese culture. Followed by *Buddha Baby* (2005).

Lee, Min Jin

⇨ *Free Food for Millionaires.* 2007. Warner. ISBN 9780446581080. 512p.

Casey Han is a first-generation Korean American dealing with the conflict between her new expensive lifestyle and her conservative immigrant family. Even though she's graduated magna cum laude from Princeton, her father kicks her out when she doesn't land a "real" job. She bunks up with a wealthy classmate and navigates the big city, from boyfriends to jobs, and works to understand her family.

Lockwood, Cara

Dixieland Sushi: A Novel. 2005. Downtown Press. ISBN 0743499425. 283p.

Japanese American Jen Nakamara Taylor hated growing up in a small Southern town, where she constantly felt like a fish out of water. She's much more secure now as an adult, living in Chicago. But all those childhood memories come back when she is summoned home to Dixieland, Arkansas, for her cousin's wedding. It doesn't help that her cousin is marrying Jen's childhood crush. Nostalgic and very funny.

Yoshikawa, Mako

Once Removed. 2003. Bantam. ISBN 0553801554. 288p.

Stepsisters and childhood friends, Jewish American Claudia and Japanese American Rei reunite after 17 years apart. When Claudia's dad married Rei's mother, friction between their mothers couldn't keep the two girls apart. What did separate them was the breakup of that second marriage. As adults, the two women reconnect when Rei develops skin cancer and turns to Claudia, who needs advice on her relationship with a married man. A quiet and sensitive portrait of a mixed family.

Yu, Michelle, and Blossom Kan
China Dolls. 2007. Thomas Dunne. 9780312362805. 288p.

Three Chinese American young women try to make it in New York City. M.J. is a successful sportswriter; Alex is a lawyer; and Lin is a stockbroker. All three are feeling pressure from their immigrant families to find love and career success. M.J. is locked out of promotions because of her gender. Alex and Lin are financially successful, but treated like "dumb girls" in their professions. The friendships and their family relationships are distinct and entertaining.

Indian American

Here's a variety of good reads featuring Indian American women dealing with the same sorts of issues any woman could face.

Banerjee, Anjali
⇨ *Imaginary Men.* 2005. Downtown Press. ISBN 1416509437. 256p.

Professional matchmaker Lina's Bengali family wants to see her quickly married off. She finds herself trapped by a lie at her sister's wedding in India, where she blurts out that she is already engaged. When she returns home to San Francisco, she searches for a boyfriend, but never sees the "shimmering thread" of romance she is famous for recognizing in other couples. When everyone clamors to meet her imaginary fiancé at the next family gathering, Lina must finally get a grip on reality. Chick lit with an authentic ethnic twist.

Daswani, Kavita
The Village Bride of Beverly Hills. 2004. Putnam. ISBN 0399152148. 271p.

Priya is very unhappy that she had to leave her family in India and move to Los Angeles with her new husband, Sanjay, mainly because Sanjay's demanding and conservative parents boss Priya around. When she doesn't get pregnant right away, her in-laws demand that she get a job to help support them. Wanting a forbidden career in journalism, Priya takes a job as a receptionist at a gossipy Hollywood magazine. When she tags along on an interview assignment, the star is smitten with her politeness and discretion, and she soon finds herself climbing the career ladder, but she must keep her new job hidden from her new family.

Divakaruni, Chitra Banerjee
Sister of My Heart. 1999. Doubleday. ISBN 0385489501. 322p.

Cousins Anju and Sudha are born on the same day in Calcutta and grow up as close as sisters. Family secrets and arranged marriages threaten to force them apart, but even Anju's move to California doesn't weaken their bond. The women narrate in alternate chapters in this moving story. Followed by *The Vine of Desire* (2002).

Malladi, Amulya
The Mango Season. 2003. Ballantine. ISBN 0345450302. 229p.

Priya goes home to India to visit her Brahmin family, who, unaware that she is engaged to an American man back in California, have chosen a "nice Indian boy" for her to marry. Scared that they will disown her, Priya goes through the elaborate charade of meeting the prospective groom and his parents. When she finally spills the beans, her family is disappointed but eventually accepting. A nuanced look at contemporary India and one woman's desire to please both herself and her family.

Mukherjee, Bharati
Jasmine. 1989. Grove Press. Reprint, 1999, Weidenfeld. ISBN 0802136303. 256p.

Jyoti, a poor Punjabi, widowed at age 17, leaves India for the United States. Her life is filled with adventure, danger, sorrow, and love. Along the journey of her life, she changes her name (several times), ends up with three children of different backgrounds, and finally settles on a farm in Iowa. An absorbing story of identity, courage, and hope.

Pradhan, Monica
The Hindi-Bindi Club. 2007. Bantam. ISBN 055338452X. 488p.

Three young women share the story in this charming novel. First-generation Americans Kiran, Preity, and Rani like to mock their Indian mothers for their old fashioned notions. The mothers simply want what they think is best for the girls—marriage to a nice Indian young man. Two cultures collide as the women find their own romances and career paths. Indian recipes, shared by the mothers, are dotted throughout the breezy narrative.

Singh, Sonia
Bollywood Confidential. 2005. Avon Trade. ISBN 0060590386. 215p.

Raveena Rai is an aspiring actress in Los Angeles. When her agent finally lands her a leading role, she's dismayed to discover it's in a Bollywood production and she'll need to travel to Bombay for the shoot. She stays in Bombay with her eccentric uncle Heeru and goes through culture shock. A fun inside look at the Indian film industry and a lighthearted tale of a young woman discovering her heritage.

Latina

Here's a variety of good reads featuring Latina women dealing with the same sorts of issues any woman could face.

Carlson, Lori M.
The Sunday Tertulia. 2000. HarperCollins. ISBN 0060195363. 208p.

Lonely New Yorker Claire strikes up a friendship with retired pharmacist Isabela, and is invited to Isabela's monthly "tertulia"—an informal gathering of women. She's the youngest and the only white woman in the group, but they welcome her just the same. The women range from Mexican doctor Aroma; Argentine intellectual Sonia; Peruvian chef Lina; among others. Lots of girl talk and an exploration of identity are the hallmarks of this novel, with poetry, recipes, and herbal remedies interspersed.

Castillo, Ana
Peel My Love Like an Onion. 1999. Doubleday. ISBN 0385496761. 213p.

Flamenco dancer Carmen Santos, a Mexican American living in Chicago, is embroiled in a love triangle when she starts to date the godson of her previous lover. But soon, the independent and passionate Carmen finds herself alone after a childhood case of polio flares up again, ending her dancing career, and the men in her life abandon her. Forced to move back in with her belittling mother, she manages to keep her spirit. An intense character study.

Castillo, Mary
In Between Men. 2006. Avon Trade. ISBN 0060766824. 304p.

When ESL teacher and single mom Isa is voted "Unsexiest Woman Alive" by her students, she thinks things can't get worse. After all, her competition included several septuagenarians! But things do get worse when her ex-husband Carlos tells a shock-jock radio DJ how bad she was in bed. Determined to be a red-hot mama, she embarks on a huge makeover. Unfortunately, she discovers that juggling a job, a young son, and her new sex-symbol status is harder than it looks. Funny and lighthearted.

Chavez, Denise
Loving Pedro Infante: A Novel. 2001. Farrar, Straus, and Giroux. ISBN 0374194114. 325p.

Thirty-something Tere Avila is a true-blue member of the Pedro Infante Club. Infante, a 1940s movie star, is the ultimate male icon—the Mexican Elvis, if you will. Tere and her friends would give anything to find someone like Pedro; their worship of Pedro leads them to a series of unfulfilling relationships and an unwillingness to move on with their lives. Peppered with plenty of Chicano slang and cultural references.

Medina, C. C.
A Little Love. 2000. Warner. ISBN 0446524484. 357p.

Four Miami Latinas rely on each other in this entertaining novel. There's Isabel, a Cuban American single mom; her ambitious cousin Mercy, a high-end real estate agent; elegant Lucinda, a Dominican American socialite; and Julia, a Mexican American professor who falls in love with another woman.

The women find and lose love, deal with various family pressures, and work out their identities.

Platas, Berta
⇨ *Cinderella Lopez.* 2006. St. Martin's Griffin. ISBN 0312341725. 277p.

Cynthia Lopez is overworked and has two evil stepsisters. Sound familiar? The three women work as VJs for a video music station, but Cyn's waiting for her 25th birthday, when she stands to inherit her late father's estate. When she meets a cute guy, she keeps him a secret fearing that her stepsisters will steal him away. Unfortunately, he turns out to be in charge of a media conglomerate set to purchase the station and leave them all out in the cold. A fun, fast-paced fairy tale with a dash of Latin spice.

Valdes-Rodriguez, Alisa
The Dirty Girls Social Club. 2003. St. Martin's. ISBN 0312313810. 304p.

Six Latina college friends from different backgrounds meet every six months to catch up and offer advice to one another. Outspoken Lauren isn't as confident as she appears; Rebecca is the founder of a popular Latina magazine; Amber is a rock musician; Elizabeth is a news anchor who's in the closet; Cuban Sara is a full-time mom; and Usnavys is a high-powered executive. A nice balance of chick lit froth and serious issues.

Sappho's Daughters: Lesbian Women's Fiction

Sensitive portrayals of lesbian women and their relationships with family, friends, and the world around them.

Anshaw, Carol
⇨ *Lucky in the Corner.* 2002. Houghton Mifflin. ISBN 0395940400. 245p.

Permanent student Fern; her lesbian mother Nora and her lover Jeanne; and her cross-dressing (straight) uncle Howard are featured in this fun novel, a look at a slightly dysfunctional but very loving family. The most stable family member is Lucky, Fern's dog. When Fern discovers her mother is cheating on Jeanne, the family dynamic is rocked. Well-paced with realistically drawn characters and great Chicago detail.

Bledsoe, Lucy Jane
Working Parts: A Novel. 1997. Seal Press. ISBN 187806794X. 195p.

Lori, a bike mechanic, has a secret—she can't read. When a friend convinces her to enroll in a literacy course, it opens up a new world for her as she struggles with the fear of exposure, which she compares to her coming-out experience. When she begins a relationship with a new girlfriend who is unaware of Lori's illiteracy, her issues deepen.

Donoghue, Emma
Landing: A Novel. 2007. Harcourt. ISBN 9780151012978. 336p.

Jude, a Canadian museum curator, meets Irish flight attendant Sile while on a flight to the United Kingdom. Despite Sile's long-term girlfriend and Jude's worries about their age difference, the women exchange letters and e-mail and begin a long-distance relationship. But when neither woman is willing to leave their home—Sile loves the big-city bustle of Dublin while Jude is attached to her tiny Ontario hometown—will they ever manage to make a relationship work?

Liebegott, Ali
The IHOP Papers. 2006. Caroll and Graff. ISBN 9780786717941. 304p.

College student Francesca follows her philosophy professor Irene to San Francisco in hopes of having a relationship with her. Free-spirited Irene isn't about to be tied down, however. Francesca takes the graveyard shift waitressing at an IHOP, working on a memoir and wishing for love. A lyrical coming-of-age story.

Meyer, Carolyn
Brown Eyes Blue. 2003. Bridge Works. ISBN 1882593685. 228p.

Dorcas is summoned to her hometown in Pennsylvania by a concerned friend, worried about Dorcas's aging artist mother, Lavinia. Lavinia's latest gallery show consists of erotic graphic nudes, a big change from her usual pastoral Amish scenes. Dorcas assesses the situation, decides Mom's not crazy, but figures she may as well stick around to keep an eye on things. When Dorcas's daughter Sasha shows up, pregnant and with a lesbian girlfriend, family secrets, old and new, are revealed. Charming, with wonderful characters.

Waters, Sarah
Tipping the Velvet. 1999. Riverhead Books. ISBN 1573221368. 472p.

In this historical novel set in Victorian England, Nan falls in love with a male impersonator, Kitty, and follows her to become part of a cross-dressing music hall act. When an ashamed Kitty marries their manager, Walter, Nancy runs away and struggles to survive the gritty streets of London. A fascinating look at the effects of a repressed era on the lives of women who dared to be different.

Songbirds

A talent showcase of female musicians.

Goldmark, Kathi Kamen
And My Shoes Keep Walking Back to You. 2002. Chronicle Books. ISBN 0811834956. 319p.

Country singer and songwriter Sarah Jean Pixlie writes a hit novelty song, which gets her kicked out of a job as a backup singer when the main star gets jealous. Heading back to her hometown in California, she tries to restart her career while dealing with an unexpected pregnancy. Witty fake country songs are interspersed, with titles such as "Credit Card Christmas" and "My Baby Used to Hold Me (Now He's Putting Me on Hold)." A fun comic read.

Kane, Carol

Diva. 1990. HarperCollins. Mass-market reissue, 1991. ISBN 0061099260. 487p.

In this sweeping novel set in the early 1900s, Moira Devereaux and her daughter, Maeve, struggle to get out of a political prison in South Africa and head for Paris, where Maeve becomes a celebrated opera star. Richly drawn scenes both in front of and behind the curtain are sure to entertain. Definitely seek out this oldie-but-goodie if you like glamorous historical fiction.

Mandel, Sally

Heart and Soul. 2002. Ballantine. ISBN 0345428927. 280p.

Piano prodigy Bess becomes an overnight success under the wing of David, a celebrated pianist. He manages to groom the tough working-class Long Island girl into a classical music diva, but he's got a dark side and a tragic past. An emotional roller coaster peppered with insight into the world of classical music.

Orloff, Erica

Diary of a Blues Goddess. 2003. Red Dress Ink. ISBN 0373250320. 296p.

Wedding singer Georgia Ray lives with her free-wheeling grandmother and drag queen best friend in a haunted former brothel in New Orleans. Georgia's actually quite successful, fronting a popular wedding band, but her real dream is to be a blues singer like her great-aunt Irene. What's holding her back? Her grandmother and friends are determined to find out, and to help her achieve her dreams.

Margolis, Sue

Breakfast at Stephanie's. 2004. Delta Trade. ISBN 0385337337. 336p.

Aspiring talented jazz singer Stephanie has a lot on her plate. Stringing together part-time jobs isn't enough to enable her to take care of her toddler son Jake. When Jake's father comes back into the picture, she's feeling torn between going back to him or sticking with a new possible romance. And what about her career?

Shortridge, Jennie

Riding with the Queen. 2003. New American Library. ISBN 0451210271. 331p.

Seventeen years after leaving home, Tallie Beck finds herself heading back home after her rock-and-roll career hits a dead end. But home doesn't have much to offer—a bipolar mother, a job she detests, and a teenage sister looking for a role model. Tallie's not quite up to dealing with any of these. And will playing the piano in a bar ever be enough of a creative outlet?

Spencer, LaVyrle
Small Town Girl. 1997. Putnam. ISBN 0399142495. 364p.

Tess McPhail, a country music superstar who left home at age 18 for Nashville, never looked back. When her mother has major surgery, she is called home to Missouri to help her siblings out. She quickly realizes no one in the tiny town of Wintergreen gives a hoot about her stardom. Slowly but surely, she manages to make friends and find romance, and even mentors a talented young girl. Charming and romantic.

Voss, Louise
⇨ *To Be Someone.* 2001. Crown. ISBN 0609608924. 389p.

Former British pop star–turned–DJ Helena is disfigured in a freak accident, and decides to do a last radio show before killing herself. Sudden and surprising success as a member of the group Blue Idea wasn't enough to save her from the grief that overwhelmed her when her best friend died of leukemia. The novel is peppered with 1980s (mostly British) pop tunes that form the emotional soundtrack of her life, as she journeys through her memory and relives her best and worst moments. Touching, absorbing, and a must for any fan of the 1980s.

All the World's a Stage

These novels feature actresses and the theatrical life.

Cohen, Leah Hager
House Lights. 2007. Norton. ISBN 9780393064513. 320p.

Young aspiring actress Beatrice contacts her estranged grandmother Margaret, a famous stage actress, in the hopes of getting career advice. When Beatrice's esteemed father is accused of sexual harassment, Beatrice runs away to Margaret, who takes the young girl under her wing. Then Beatrice is cast in a summer stock production, and she falls in love with a much older theater director, learns more about what strained the relationship between her mother and grandmother, and begins to come to terms with the dysfunction in her family.

Delbanco, Francesca
Ask Me Anything. 2004. Norton. ISBN 0393051706. 256p.

Rosalie is an advice columnist for a teen magazine by day, actress by night. After college, she moved to New York with a acting troupe of friends looking to launch their careers, but none of them have really made it yet and they're all drifting apart. Friendships are further strained when two of the group fall in love with each other, and Rosalie begins an affair with one of their fathers. When another actor from the troupe lands a new play by a hot Irish playwright, it just might push Rosalie right over the edge into a quarter-life crisis.

Heller, Jane
Lucky Stars. 2003. St. Martin's. ISBN 0312288484. 306p.

Aspiring Hollywood actress Stacey can't believe her domineering mother Helen has one-upped her yet again. After complaining to a tuna company about a bone in her last can, Helen manages to impress the company so much that they give her the starring role in their latest major ad campaign, and quickly becomes a sought-after character actress. Meanwhile Stacey toils away at local commercials and part-time retail jobs. How fair is that?! Mom moves to Los Angeles and falls in love with a smooth talker, leaving Stacey at her wit's end in this funny and fresh novel.

Martin, Beverly S.
Juffie Kane. 1989. Bantam. ISBN 0553053450. 504p.

Juffie grows up in the 1930s as the beloved granddaughter of gangsters, Dino and Bennie. In the 1940s, when her acting career was going nowhere fast, she entered into a deal with the Mob. By the time she's 25, she's had a string of Broadway hits, but is "owned" by a gangster who forces her to play Vegas and act as a dope courier. She's at the peak of her career by the time the 1950s roll around, but is killed in an avalanche in Switzerland—or is she? Characters that jump off the page and all of the glitz and glamour of an actress's life make this older title absolutely worth seeking out, especially if you like steamy sagas with strong heroines.

Michel, DeLauné
The Safety of Secrets. 2008. HarperCollins. ISBN 0060817364. 320p.

Fiona and Patricia have been best friends since first grade. They move to Los Angeles to become actresses, and remain close even as their paths diverge. Fiona is a fairly successful actress, happier being married and expecting a child instead of being a star, while Patricia catapults to stardom as the host of a sports reality show. When Patricia impulsively marries a handsome movie star, Fiona is unsure if they have anything in common anymore. Things only get worse when Patricia reveals a secret the two have been keeping since their teens.

Nathan, Melissa
Pride, Prejudice, and Jasmin Field. 2001. HarperCollins. ISBN 0060184957. 280p.

Jasmin Field's life is unraveling. Her magazine column is failing, and her best friend has just moved away. Winning the lead role of Elizabeth Bennet in a charity performance of *Pride and Prejudice* just might cheer her up, though, especially since Darcy is played by a Hollywood hunk, albeit a real jerky hunk. Cleverly follows much of the original work's storylines.

Shaffer, Louise

➪ *Family Acts.* 2007. Ballantine. ISBN 9781400060634. 336p.

Complete strangers Katie and Randa find themselves joint inheritors of a famous but crumbling theater, the Venerable Opera house, in small-town Georgia. As they unravel their shared history and the history of the theater, readers are treated to a rich, delightful back story involving a talented acting family, love, betrayal, and secrets.

Chapter Three

Setting

Setting is the where and the when of a story, and in women's fiction is generally not as relevant as the story itself or the characters.

Deep South to New York City; from the playgrounds of the rich and famous to the kitchens of the average cook; and from historical settings to the present day.

Brit Lit

Surely you've read the one who started the craze, *Bridget Jones*? Now venture across the pond and meet her British friends.

Adams, Carrie
The Godmother. 2007. HarperCollins. ISBN 0755329546. 400p.

Tessa is godmother to four of her friend's children, but desperately wants to be married and have her own family. At least she thinks she does. She's really not sure whether she's ready to give up her swinging London social life full of one-night stands. Besides, her one true love, a man she's been in love with since they were teens, is already married. And when she takes a careful look around at her married friends, Tessa begins to see that they aren't living such perfect lives. So what's a single girl to do? Perhaps she's better off just a godmother, after all.

Green, Jane
⇨ *Jemima J.* 2001. Broadway. ISBN 9780767905183. 384p.

Jemima is the office ugly duckling—overweight and plain. Desperate to gain the confidence to get to know her cute workmate, she starts off with

Internet dating, figuring she can gain some social skills while hiding behind an online persona. When her American online pal wants to meet, she embarks on a rigorous makeover. A delightful look at the cultural differences (and similarities) between America and Great Britain.

Holden, Wendy
Bad Heir Day. 2001. Plume. ISBN 9780452281783. 352p.

Aspiring writer Anna gets dumped by her boyfriend and vows to throw herself into her career. Unaware that the job really means being the nanny for Cassandra's spoiled brat son, she takes a job as a writer's assistant for Cassandra, a social-climbing author with a rock star husband. Desperate to escape the situation, Anna starts dating Jamie, the heir to a Scottish castle, but is he all he's cracked up to be? Holden has a keen comic eye for over-the-top yet realistic characters, and the Scottish scenes are damp enough to leave mold on your bookmark.

Keyes, Marian
Lucy Sullivan is Getting Married. 2002. Avon. ISBN 9780060090371. 624p.

Or is she? A fortune teller predicts Lucy will be married within a year, but with no romantic prospects in her life, Lucy is pretty skeptical. All of a sudden, she starts meeting all kinds of eligible men...but which one is right for her? Family issues with her alcoholic father complicate her life further. Keyes is the undisputed queen of U.K. chick lit, and this novel has great London flavor.

Kinsella, Sophie
Can You Keep A Secret? 2005. Dial. ISBN 9780385338080. 384p.

A stand-alone title from the author of the fluffy and funny *Shopaholic* series. Emma has a seemingly perfect boyfriend and is up for a promotion at her seemingly perfect job. On a turbulent plane ride back from a terrible client meeting, Emma fears for her life, and she spills her most intimate secrets, including the fact that she hates her job, to the handsome man sitting next to her. After a safe landing and back at work, she discovers he's her new boss. Kinsella perfectly captures the British office environment.

Wickham, Madeline
Cocktails for Three. 2001. St. Martin's. ISBN 0312281927. 300p.

Candice, Maggie, and Roxanne are work pals who meet up in London for cocktails on the first of every month to dissect their current situations. Roxanne is having a heated affair, Maggie is a new mom with an unsympathetic mother-in-law and distant husband, and Candice has a guilty secret. When scheming Heather enters the mix, the friendships are tested. (Wickham also writes funnier, fluffier chick lit as Sophie Kinsella.)

Wolff, Isabel
The Trials of Tiffany Trott. 1998. Onyx. ISBN 0451408888. 404p.

Desperate to find Mr. Right, Tiffany does everything from answering personal ads, signing up with dating agencies, and blind dates, but she keeps meeting disaster after disaster. Funny, sexy and saucy, with plenty of British flavor.

The Rich Are Different

See how the other side lives in these glam and glitz novels.

Bagshawe, Louise
For All the Wrong Reasons. 2002. St. Martin's. ISBN 0312272553. 325p.

Wealthy snob Diana spends her days gossiping, shopping, and hostessing the most fabulous New York parties. When she discovers her husband's been cheating on her, all hell breaks loose; and once the vicious divorce is over, she's left without a penny. What's a former socialite to do? Why, have a steamy affair with her blue collar new boss, of course!

Bagshawe, Tilly
Adored. 2005. Warner. ISBN 0446576883. 560p.

Siena McMahon is the glamorous granddaughter of Hollywood movie legend Duke McMahon. Gorgeous, talented, and ambitious, Siena is on the path to stardom, but obstacles such as illegitimate relatives, jealousy, and, yes, true love, keep getting in her way. A sexy, juicy blockbuster and a great beach read.

Collins, Jackie
Hollywood Wives. 1983. Simon & Schuster. Reprint, 1987, Pocket. ISBN 0671704591. 560p.
Hollywood Wives: The New Generation. 2001. Simon & Schuster. ISBN 0743216342. 833p.

Collins revved up the world of glitz and glamour novels with her 1983 novel *Hollywood Wives,* the story of Hollywood heavyweights and their personal dramas, heavy on the adultery, jealousy, and secrets. She followed with *Hollywood Wives: The New Generation,* adding more contemporary details as well as more drama. In both, plenty of money, celebrities, steamy sex, drugs, and the high life abound—perfect escapism.

Gould, Judith
The Secret Heiress. 2006. New American Library. ISBN 045121966X. 320p.

Niki Papadaki, an international party girl, inherits a multimillion dollar corporate empire. Her lack of any business sense and wild-child ways infuriate the board, however, and she is well on her way to destroying the company. Then Niki's separated-at-birth twin sister, Ariadne, appears out of the blue to save the day and the fortune. Over-the-top fun and decadence.

Graves, Lindsay
To Catch a Husband. 2006. Ballantine. ISBN 0345485483. 288p.

Four women living in a mega-rich gated California community bond over their bitter divorces. They spend their days drinking expensive wine, comparing plastic surgeries, and driving fancy cars. So who needs husbands? Well, a new husband would certainly break up the monotony of art galleries and charity functions. When they all fall for the same billionaire, the claws come out.

Krantz, Judith
Dazzle. 1990. Crown. Reprint, 1994, Bantam. ISBN 0553293761. 592p.

Jazz is a famous celebrity photographer, owner of the Hollywood photography studio Dazzle. Her life is an endless loop of drama—she's caught between two men, her ex-fiancé is back on the scene, her half-sisters hate her, and she's fighting for control of her father's immense land holdings. Sex, celebrity, and money—who could ask for more?

Strohmeyer, Sarah
⇨*The Secret Lives of Fortunate Wives.* 2005. Dutton. ISBN 0525949097. 349p.

This campy novel features the denizens of an exclusive Cleveland gated community, Hunting Hills. McMansions, platinum AmEx cards, and shallow trophy wives abound. When socially awkward Claire marries into the mix, she finds herself dodging odd social norms and scandals. The exploits of these desperate housewives will make you laugh and groan.

Thomas, Heather
Trophies. 2008. William Morrow. ISBN 9780061126246. 528p.

Their husbands may be the most powerful entertainment executives in Hollywood, but the wives are the ones who really run the show. Five women with nothing in common but their lavish, mega-rich lifestyles. These characters worry about everything from losing their fortunes if they get dumped to climbing to the top of the social heap. This fictional look at over-the-top Hollywood lives is as satirical as it gets.

In a Different Time

These books transport you to a different time and place, with lavish detail and true-to-life characters.

Baker, Ellen

⇨*Keeping the House.* 2007. Random House. ISBN 1400066352. 544p.

Baker does double duty, telling the story of a family from 1896 through the end of World War I, and the parallel story of a woman named Dolly bucking convention in the 1950s. Dolly, a free spirit, doesn't have much in common with the coffee klatch women in the small Wisconsin town her husband has dragged her to live in. She becomes obsessed with the abandoned mansion on the hill and the family secrets hidden there. Both stories showcase fine detail of their respective time periods and the social mores of the day.

Binchy, Maeve

Circle of Friends. 1991. Delacorte. ISBN 0783108346. 565p.

Binchy transports readers to a 1950s Irish village to tell the story of Benny, overweight and shy; her best friend Eve, an orphan; and a host of colorful local characters. The girls grow up and endure the conservative decade, heartbreak, and betrayal of friends. More than just a charming coming-of-age tale filled with memorable characters, *Circle of Friends* captures the religious and social flavor of Ireland in the 1950s with almost picture-perfect detail.

Clayton, Meg Waite

The Wednesday Sisters. 2008. Ballantine. ISBN 0345502825. 288p.

Set during the summer of 1968, in this novel captures a turbulent era in American history, as seen through the eyes of five women who meet for a weekly writing group. Linda is an athlete with a health scare, Frankie dreams of becoming famous writer, Ally is dealing with fertility issues in an age before infertility treatments. The women's friendship blossoms as they help each other through life's challenges, and Clayton evokes a real sense of America on the cusp of social change.

Domingue, Ronlyn

The Mercy of Thin Air. 2005. Atria. ISBN 0743278801. 320p.

Raziela Nolan, the outspoken and brazen belle of 1920s New Orleans, tragically drowns in a accident. Her spirit stays around though, in the "thin air"—a kind of in-between-world—for nearly 80 years, keeping watch among the living. She is a haunted ghost, not one who haunts—her true love Andrew has disappeared under her watch and she misses him. Raziela's story unfolds in flashbacks and remembrances of the 1920s. Not just a romantic and heart-breaking storyteller, Domingue paints a lush and richly detailed picture of an unconventional life in the 1920s.

Haigh, Jennifer

Baker Towers. 2005. William Morrow. ISBN 0060509414. 352p.

Haigh paints an evocative picture of a mining town in post–World War II Pennsylvania. After their father dies, the children of the Italian Polish Novak family try to escape their dreary life. Mother Rose struggles but can never escape the narrow-mindedness that goes along with small town life. Much more than a family story, Haigh captures the hardscrabble era with grace and sympathy.

Kabak, Carrie
Cover the Butter. 2005. Dutton. ISBN 0525948767. 368p.

Middle-aged housewife Kate revisits her life coming of age in Britain in the 1970s through becoming a wife and mother in the 1980s. Pushed around by an overbearing and controlling mother, she gets married to an insensitive man. When her teenage son trashes her beloved home, she realizes it's time to stand up for herself and not become a victim of bad choices. Along with this story of empowerment, readers get a detailed journey through the turbulent latter half of the century.

Kagan, Leslie
Whistling in the Dark. 2007. NAL Accent. ISBN 0451221230. 320p.

In this coming-of-age tale set in Milwaukee, Wisconsin, in the 1950s, sisters Sally and Troo are left to their own devices when their mother is hospitalized for hepatitis. Their stepfather is too drunk to take care of them, and eventually abandons the girls along with their older sister, who is interested more in her boyfriends than her little sisters. The girls spend much of their free time worrying about the neighborhood and the people around them, as they fear a child predator is on the loose. Kagan is a talented writer and evokes a *Wonder Years* sense of a Midwest industrial city in the late 1950s.

Landvik, Lorna
Oh My Stars. 2005. Ballantine. ISBN 0345472314. 400p.

During the Depression, shy Violet runs away from her boring life and abusive father and ends up with a musical motley crew touring the country. She becomes the manager of the Pearltones, a racially mixed rockabilly band. A fun, musical romp with colorful characters, but also a finely drawn portrait of the United States in the 1930s, particularly the divided South.

McGraw, Erin
The Seamstress of Hollywood Boulevard. 2008. Houghton Mifflin. ISBN 0618386289. 384p.

Nell Platt grew up poor in Mercer County, Kansas. Only 17, she's already married to escape her bleak farm life but finds she's traded one sad situation for another. A talented seamstress, she decides to leave her husband and two baby daughters behind, and runs away to Hollywood. Once there, she quickly establishes herself as a master seamstress and invents a whole new persona. Twenty years later, her daughters show up on her doorstep, demanding answers. Based on her grandmother's life, McGraw seamlessly moves from rural Kansas circa 1900 to the glittering streets of California in the 1920s.

Morton, Kate
The House at Riverton. 2008. Atria. ISBN 9781416550518. 480p.

This atmospheric tale introduces 99-year-old Grace Reeves, who is forced to look back at her life and remember dangerous secrets involving the English family she worked for as a maid between the two world wars. At 14, Grace was sent to Riverton to work for the aristocratic Ashbury family. As time progressed, she learned of family secrets, including one involving herself, became a lady's maid to the two Ashbury sisters, and got caught in the middle of scandal. A rich look at England between the wars, and an engrossing portrait of a woman trapped by deceit and the uncertainty of where her life will take her.

Trigiani, Adriana
Lucia Lucia. 2003. Random House. ISBN 1400060052. 256p.

Greenwich Village in the 1950s is the colorful setting for this novel. Lucia, a good Italian girl, strikes out on her own in New York, working as a talented department store seamstress and bucking convention, when her fiancée and his mother expected her to quit working and become a meek wife and mother. The Village of the 1950s is a character in it's own right in this richly detailed story.

Single in the City

More than just chick lit dating stories, these novels capture the energy and personality of a big city.

Brodsky, Danielle
Princess of Park Avenue. 2005. Berkley Trade. ISBN 0425205371. 352p.

Lorraine Machuchi loves living in her close-knit Brooklyn neighborhood, but is getting weary of pining over Tommy, a local guy who tells her she's "going nowhere." Determined to get "somewhere," she crosses the bridge to Manhattan and decides she wants to be just like the women she meets every day at her new job in a swanky salon—pampered and primped to the nines. Which girl is she meant to be—a brassy Brooklynite or a Park Avenue Princess? A loving look at the many different faces of New York.

Brown, Josie
True Hollywood Lies. 2005. Avon Trade. ISBN 0060815876. 310p.

Hannah is the down-to-earth daughter of a Hollywood actor. When her famous father dies and her evil stepmother freezes her trust fund, she takes a job as personal assistant for heartthrob Louis Trollope, and spends her time ordering him Zone-diet meals and arranging his many trysts with starlets. A fun look at the Hollywood scene.

Caldwell, Laura
Clean Slate. 2003. Red Dress Ink. ISBN 037325038X. 312p.

Chicagoan Kelly discovers she has inexplicably lost her memories of the last five months. Everywhere she goes, she discovers the life she knew no longer exists. She decides maybe she's better off that way, and embarks on a new journey. True Chicago details surround this mysterious tale of a woman struggling to make sense of her past, present, and future.

Keyes, Marian
⇨ *Angels.* 2002. William Morrow. ISBN 0060008024. 352p.

Moving out of her usual Irish territory, Keyes follows Walsh sister Maggie to sunny Los Angeles. Maggie's not used to the complicated social scene of trendy Los Angeles, not to mention all the sunshine. Her best friend, a struggling screenwriter, takes her under her wing and introduces her to California culture, superficial though it may be.

Langston, Cynthia
Bicoastal Babe. 2006. New American Library. ISBN 0451218450. 313p.

First Lindsey gets to escape the suburbs for a high-powered ad job in Chicago. As if that big city wasn't enough, she soon finds herself jetting between Manhattan and Los Angeles, juggling a hotshot Wall Street broker on one coast and a laid-back surfer dude on the other. Vivid descriptions of each city mean it doesn't get more big-city than this.

Pace, Alison
Pug Hill. 2006. Berkley. ISBN 0425209717. 312p.

Art restorer Hope McNeill spends her free time at Central Park's Pug Hill, despite not owning a dog herself. The playful dogs give her the unconditional love and freedom she feels her life lacks. To break out of her shyness, she signs up for a public speaking class and comes across a flaky cast of characters. You'll feel like you're right there in Central Park and the Metropolitan Museum of Art while reading about Hope's adventures as a shy girl in the big city.

Papa, Ariella
Up and Out. 2003. Red Dress Ink. ISBN 0373250428. 315p.

Rebecca Cole works in TV production and has created a lovable cartoon character. When her company is bought by a bank (of all things) all hell breaks loose and she doesn't know what to do as she begins to lose control of her creation. Almost too "New York" for it's own good, Rebecca's adventures in the big city give a real taste of the New York scene, from apartments to dining.

Senate, Melissa
See Jane Date. 2001. Red Dress Ink. ISBN 0373250118. 283p.

Jane has two months to find a date for her cousin's wedding, and that's the least of her woes. She lives in a typically cramped and expensive New York

City apartment, and an unfulfilling job as an assistant editor for Posh Publishing. Real New York flavor sets this chick lit fare out of the crowd.

Yardley, Cathy

L.A. Woman. 2002. Red Dress Ink. ISBN 0373250169. 285p.

Sarah Walker moves from her small California town to Los Angeles for her boyfriend. When they break up, she becomes committed to transforming into a true "L.A. Woman," a club-hopping, fancy-free single gal. Fresh West Coast flavor, perfectly capturing the glamour (and gritty underbelly) of the Los Angeles scene.

The South Shall Rise Again

Southern belles, at their best (and worst!). These novels have as much Southern flavor as fried chicken and shoofly pie.

Des Pres, Lorraine

⇨ *The Scandalous Summer of Sissy LeBlanc.* 2001. William Morrow. ISBN 0688173896. 342p.

Nothing ever happens in Gentry, Louisiana. Bored housewife Sissy Le-Blanc is dissatisfied with her life. When her high school boyfriend Parker comes back to town during the summer of 1956, her sneaky kids catch her kissing him, and decide to blackmail her. As if that wasn't bad enough, Parker's girlfriend is Sissy's secret cousin, and that's only the beginning of the scandalous family secrets.

Flagg, Fannie

Daisy Fay and the Miracle Man. 1992. Warner. ISBN 0446394521. 320p.

Small-town Mississippi in the 1950s is the setting for this coming-of-age tale. Daisy Fay Harper's diary begins in 1952 when she is a precocious 11-year-old; and the diary ends in 1959 when she wins the Miss Mississippi pageant and leaves Mississippi for a New York acting career. Along the way we are treated to a host of crazy characters. Flagg has a knack for capturing the feel and flavor of the Deep South, and her wacky characters are never stock stereotypes—they have heart.

Gayle, Stephanie

My Summer of Southern Discomfort. 2007. William Morrow. ISBN 0061236292. 256p.

Young New York lawyer Natalie Goldberg takes a job at a Georgia law firm in order to escape the city and a failed affair with a coworker. She gets more than she bargained for when she is assigned to a death penalty case, which goes against the grain of her Yankee liberalism. Funny and poignant,

Gayle has the pages positively dripping with her descriptions of a humid Southern summer.

Gillespie, Karin

Bet Your Bottom Dollar: A Bottom Dollar Girls Novel. **Bottom Dollar Girls.** 2004. Simon & Schuster. ISBN 0743250109. 304p.

In this first book of the series, Elizabeth manages a local general store, the Bottom Dollar Emporium in Cayboo Creek, South Carolina. When a corporate chain threatens the business, wanting to move in, Elizabeth and her two partners, widow Mavis and dotty 80-year-old Attalee, try to save the store. But her quirky family and even quirkier love life keep getting in the way.

Lippi, Rosina

Tied to the Tracks. 2006. Putnam. ISBN 9780399153495. 304p.

Documentary filmmaker Angelina is hired by a Georgia college to produce a movie about prominent faculty member and literary celebrity Zula Bragg. Coincidentally, Angelina's ex-boyfriend John happens to be on the faculty. She's ready to be professional, but local busybodies are ready to run with the story of her arrival. Will that put the brakes on John's upcoming wedding? Lippi portrays a picturesque Deep South town with plenty of quirky characters.

Moyer, Marsha

The Second Coming of Lucy Hatch. 2002. William Morrow. ISBN 0060081651. 291p.

Moyer peppers her story with plenty of authentic country twang. When young widow Lucy Hatch returns to Mooney, Texas, her sister-in-law Geneva makes it her business to see that Lucy gets back into the social scene at the local honky-tonk, the Round Up. Followed by two more Lucy Hatch novels: *The Last of the Honky Tonk Angels* (2003) and *Heartbreak Town* (2007).

Ocean, T. Lynn

Sweet Home Carolina. 2006. Thomas Dunne. ISBN 0312343345. 272p.

Young PR exec Jaxie loves her big-city life in Atlanta. So she's less than thrilled when her boss sends her to rural South Carolina on a pro bono mission to revitalize the cachet of his hometown. When Jaxie discovers the town's pirate-filled past, she hatches a plan to lure in the tourists. But a casino-building developer and an impending hurricane may derail her plans.

Siddons, Anne Rivers

Nora, Nora. 2000. HarperCollins. ISBN 006017613X. 263p.

In this novel set in 1960s Georgia, Peyton McKenzie is the self-appointed leader of the Losers Club. The other members are Boot, the grandson of the black housekeeper who works for Peyton's father; and Ernie, the eccentric sexton of the Methodist church. Not exactly the kind of friends a young teen girl generally has or needs. When Peyton's outspoken and independent older cousin, Nora, arrives for the summer, she turns Peyton's world upside down with her liberal views. A great slice of life novel that perfectly captures the socially and racially charged South of the 1960s.

White, Bailey
Quite a Year for Plums. 1998. Knopf. ISBN 0679445315. 220p.

In a fictional southern Georgia town, retired schoolteachers Hilma and Meade fret over their neighbors. In particular, there's Roger, a peanut scientist, who falls in love with Della, an artist who paints chickens. Meanwhile, Roger's ex-mother-in-law tries to communicate with martians. And she's not even the most eccentric one in town. A gentle and humorous read.

Our Town

Even if you're from the big city, you'll feel at home in these charming small towns.

Adams, Alice
A Southern Exposure. 1995. Knopf. ISBN 0679444521. 305p.

During the Depression, the Bairds and their young daughter move to the small town of Pinehill, North Carolina. Thinking they will be seen as glamorous big-city folks, they are surprised when they have to work very hard to enter the strict communal hierarchy; and they struggle to understand the rules of small-town life. Small-town gossip is at its best (or would that be, worst?) in this novel.

Baumbich, Charlene
Dearest Dorothy, Who Would Have Ever Thought? Dearest Dorothy Series. 2005. Penguin. ISBN014303619X. 340p.

In this fourth entry of the Dearest Dorothy series (beginning with *Dearest Dorothy, Are We There Yet?,* 2004) the quirky inhabitants of Partonville, Illinois, prepare for the Thanksgiving holiday. Bossy acting mayor Gladys wears down people's patience, motel manager Jessica Joy deals with an unexpected crisis, and real-estate mogul Katie plans to turn the town into a tourist destination. Meanwhile, matriarch Dorothy watches over all.

Binchy, Maeve
Whitethorn Woods. 2007. Knopf. ISBN 9780307265781. 352p.

The residents of tiny Irish village Rossmore band together when a planned highway threatens to cut through their beloved Whitethorn Woods, which means the destruction of St. Ann's Well, a shrine thought to deliver miracles. With stories spanning generations, Binchy shows some of her best character work and gets the intimacies of small-town life spot-on.

Delinsky, Barbara

Lake News. 1999. Simon & Schuster. ISBN 0684864320. 380p.

When a reporter unjustly accuses Lily Blake of having had an affair with a newly appointed Catholic cardinal, the cabaret singer retreats to her rural home town of Lake Henry, New Hampshire. Hoping to find refuge from the press, she finds herself forging a friendship with the editor of the local paper instead. And unfortunately, the town is still whispering about the youthful indiscretions in her past.

Flagg, Fannie

Can't Wait to Get to Heaven. 2006. Random House. ISBN 9781400061266. 352p.

When 80-year-old Elner Shimfissle falls out of a fig tree, she makes her way up in Heaven, where her cranky sister awaits. As Elner tries to adjust to life after death, the close-knit small town of Elmwood Springs attempts to adjust to losing one of their favorite residents. Different characters get to speak their minds in short vignettes, interspersed with Elner's heavenly findings.

King, Cassandra

Making Waves. 2004. Hyperion. ISBN 9780786887934. 285p.

Donnette Sullivan recently inherited her aunt's old house and beauty shop in the small town of Clarksville, Alabama. Her husband, Tim, has been injured in a car accident, derailing a promising football career. Most folks in town don't think he belongs painting signs for a beauty shop, and some folks don't even think the couple belongs together. King gives us a clear vision of Southern culture and small-town life.

Letts, Billie

Where the Heart Is. 1995. Warner. ISBN 0446519723. 358p.

Teenage Novalee, pregnant and abandoned by her boyfriend, finds herself stranded in a Wal-mart in tiny Sequoyah, Oklahoma. When the eccentric locals discover her, they take her in as one of their own. A quirky and loveable cast of characters, from religious convert Sister Husband to wise black photographer Moses Whitecotton, round out this story of unexpected family and the powerful bonds that can form between strangers.

Matlock, Curtiss Ann

Sweet Dreams at the Goodnight Motel. **Valentine Series.** 2004. Mira. ISBN 9780778320913. 384p.

This is Matlock's sixth book set in the small town of Valentine, Oklahoma (the first was *Lost Highway,* 1999). After a bitter divorce, Claire Wilder visits her father in Valentine. Intending to stay just a few days, complications arise and she finds herself stuck there for the summer. The town's eccentric residents take her in as one of their own, meddling in her life as much as they do with everyone else's life! Matlock's Valentine series of books share the same small town, but very different stories.

Ní Aonghusa, Clair
Civil and Strange. 2008. Houghton Mifflin. ISBN 9780618829361. 320p.

When Ellen, a 38-year-old teacher from Dublin, escapes her failed marriage and returns to her family's small Irish village, she hopes to recapture the warm feelings of her childhood. Instead, she must deal with eccentric characters and small-town gossip. Ellen decides to renovate her late aunt's crumbling home, much to the interest of the locals. When she attracts the attention of the handsome young contractor, tongues wag. An interesting portrait of modern rural Ireland.

Trigiani, Adriana
⇨ *Big Stone Gap.* 2000. Random House. ISBN 0375504036. 272p.

Small-town pharmacist Ave Maria is well-liked and well-respected in her tiny town of Big Stone Gap, Virginia, but even though she was born and raised in Big Stone Gap, she is considered a foreigner simply because her mother is Italian. When her mother dies, she finds out her real father is not who she thought. Her many friends in town rally around her and provide comic relief. Trigiani perfectly captures a snapshot of life in a small Appalachian town.

What's Cooking?

Even if your interest in food leans more towards takeout than gourmet, these books appeal with their delicious depictions of restaurants, caterers, bakeries, and other culinary delights.

Andrews, Mary Kay
⇨ *Deep Dish.* 2008. HarperCollins. ISBN 9780060837365. 384p.

TV chef Gina is up for a national show on the Cooking Channel. Her rival is the handsome but annoying host of a redneck cooking show for men, known as Tate "Kill It and Grill It" Moody. The sparks fly as does the hilarity when the two battle it out for their final chance at stardom, while dealing with their own families and personal issues. Andrews writes characters with a perfect balance of humor and depth, and just enough romance to round the story out.

Binchy, Maeve
Quentins. 2002. Dutton. ISBN 0525946829. 352p.

Dublin's favorite (fictional) hometown restaurant, Quentins, is being featured in a documentary movie. Ella, having been jilted and robbed of her savings by a scheming boyfriend, throws herself into helping her filmmaker friends cover the beloved restaurant. Talking with patrons, chefs, waitstaff, and neighbors, she collects 30 years of stories from locals and loyal patrons in this charming read.

Criswell, Millie
The Trouble with Mary. 2001. Ivy Books. ISBN 0804119503. 308p.

Mary sets out to open a restaurant in Baltimore's Little Italy, but her family's constant interference complicates things. To top it all off, she falls in love with a local food critic who has given her a bad review. Humor and romance abound, but Mary's eccentric family is at the heart of this story—as well as delicious Italian recipes.

Fforde, Katie

Second Thyme Around. 2001. St. Martin's. ISBN 0312273045. 371p.

Perdita, an organic gardener, hates being the center of attention. Her ex-husband, Lucas, a talented but hot-headed chef, is set to star in a new cooking show, and he wants Perdita to co-host. Sparks fly, but Perdita also has to juggle the ailing Kitty, the elderly woman who's been a second mother to her. Lovely characters and a charming, often humorous story.

Hammond, Diane

Going to Bend. 2004. Doubleday. ISBN 038550943X. 400p.

Petie and Rose are two friends struggling to make ends meet in small-town Oregon supplying homemade soup for the new cafe in town, Souperior. Their lives are poor in money and material goods, but rich in friendship. When their employer presses them to write a cookbook, their fortunes may turn. Can their friendship withstand the change?

Hendricks, Judith Ryan

Bread Alone. 2001. William Morrow. ISBN 0060188952. 358p.

When her husband leaves her for another woman, Wynter decides it's time for a new life. She leaves Los Angeles and moves to Seattle to take a job in a bakery, where she rediscovers her passion for breadmaking. Followed by the sequel, *The Baker's Apprentice* (2005), this winsome novel of a woman finding herself amidst the sweet scent of baked goods also includes bread recipes.

Hinton, Lynne

Friendship Cake. **Hope Springs Series.** 2000. Harper. ISBN 9780688171476. 210p.

The Hope Springs Community Church women's group is eclectic, at best. Beatrice is the town gossip; Louise is tough on the outside but ready to crack; young Charlotte is the new pastor. When the women get together to create a community cookbook, they realize they can be friends despite seemingly having nothing in common. Homestyle country-cookbook recipes are included.

Kalpakian, Laura

American Cookery: A Novel. 2006. St. Martin's. ISBN 0312348118. 288p.

Independent spirit Eden was born into a strict Mormon family, but decided to follow her own, unconventional path. Food plays an important part in her story, as the novel features over two dozen recipes that figure prominently in different stages of Eden's life, from her adventures in Europe during World War II to feeding her family at weddings, funerals, and other gatherings.

Kline, Christina Baker
The Way Life Should Be. 2007. William Morrow. ISBN 0060798912. 288p.

Angela is dissatisfied with her job, Manhattan, and life in general. On a whim after finding a man on an online dating site who lives in Maine, she packs it all up and moves to the coast of Maine, only to discover both the man and the area were not what she was expecting. Determined to make the best of things, she rents a cottage, takes a job at the local coffee hangout, and begins teaching cooking classes. Homestyle Italian recipes are included.

MacDowell, Heather, and Rose MacDowell
Turning Tables. 2008. Dial. ISBN 9780385338561. 336p.

When Erin loses her high-powered marketing position, she pulls some strings to get a job as a waitress for Roulette, a top New York restaurant. One problem—she's got no experience, and this shows loud and clear from her inability to get orders straight to her slip up of getting drunk during the restaurant's wine seminar. Juggling two men doesn't help matters much, and neither does her quest to find out what she really wants to do with life—all she knows is, it's not waitressing. Written by industry-insider sisters, this is a fun and fast-paced look at the upscale restaurant scene.

Prunty, Morag
Recipes for a Perfect Marriage. 2006. Hyperion. 1401301975. 306p.

Only two months after marrying Dan, cookbook author Tressa comes to the terrible conclusion that she isn't in love with him. She wishes her grandmother Bernadine, who taught her to cook, was still around—she learned so much about love from her grandmother's seemingly perfect marriage. When she comes across Bernadine's diaries from the 1930s and 1940s, she begins to realize that nothing is ever perfect. Seems you can't hurry love, just as you can't expect the dough to rise on your timetable. Old-fashioned Irish recipes are interspersed throughout.

Ray, Jeanne
Eat Cake. 2002. Shaye Areheart Books. ISBN 060961004X. 240p.

Ruth finds baking a relaxing escape from the troubles of everyday life. Her husband just lost his job, her estranged father is coming to live with them while he recuperates from an injury, and her teen daughter is getting moodier by the minute. Baking is the one thing she can indulge in, and she often pretends she's looking at the world from inside a nice soft layer of cake. Delicious recipes round out this sweet story.

Strohmeyer, Sarah
Sweet Love. 2008. Dutton. ISBN 0525950648. 320p.

Julie, a 40-something journalist and single mom, is happy enough living in a duplex above her mother, Elizabeth. Elizabeth is not happy that her daughter has no love life, and, regretting forcing her daughter to dump her first love Michael, surreptitiously signs the ex-sweethearts up for a cooking class so they can rekindle their relationship. Problem is, Michael and Julie have crossed paths before, when Julie wrote a scathing report on Michael's politician boss, ruining the careers of both men. Will crème brûlée and a dessert called Chocolate Orgasm be enough to help the pair reconcile?

Queens of the Wild Frontier

Classic tales of pioneer women making a go of it in the unchartered West in the 1800s.

Dallas, Sandra
The Diary of Mattie Spencer. 1997. St. Martin's. ISBN 0312187106. 229p.

Plain Mattie leaves Iowa in a Conestoga wagon with her handsome husband in 1865 for the Colorado Territories. She's dismayed by her new sod home, but is determined to make the best of it, since she still can't quite believe her luck at marrying such a catch. Dallas captures wonderful details about frontier life along with finely drawn characters.

Gloss, Molly
The Jump-Off Creek. 1989. Houghton Mifflin. ISBN 0395510864. 186p.

Lydia leaves her home in Pennsylvania for frontier life in the high mountains of Oregon. She's leaving behind memories of a disappointing marriage for the freedom of the West. The struggles of survival bring Lydia and her neighbors together. Details of the rituals of pioneer life abound in this spare novel.

Holland, Cecelia
An Ordinary Woman: A Dramatized Biography of Nancy Kelsey. 1999. Forge. ISBN 0312865287. 223p.

Holland uses letters and archival material to recreate the life of pioneer woman Nancy Kelsey, the first American woman to reach California. Nancy and her husband Ben travel by horse and on foot across an uncharted course across the country from Missouri to California across the Sierra Nevada, encountering hostile Native Americans, bad weather, and illness. Upon reaching California, they take over the land in the Bear Flag Rebellion.

Landis, Jill Marie
Summer Moon. 2001. Ballantine. ISBN 0345440390. 404p.

Approaching spinsterhood, schoolteacher Kate answers the newspaper ad of a widowed Texas rancher looking for a mail-order bride. When she arrives in Texas to meet her new husband, Reed, she's shocked to discover he apparently didn't order her. He's been too busy searching for his young son, kidnapped by Comanche Indians five years ago. Turns out Reed's father placed the ad and corresponded with Kate. He agrees to take her in, however, once he realizes she'd make a fine mother for his rescued son.

Turner, Nancy

➪ *These is My Words: The Diary of Sarah Agnes Prine.* **Sarah Agnes Prine Novels.** 1998. ReganBooks. ISBN 0060392258. 384p.

Based on Turner's great-grandmother's diaries, this is the story of a strong woman living in the Arizona Territories in the late 1800s. Uneducated Sarah overcomes her poor beginnings and lives through attacks by Indians and outlaws, outbreaks of disease, love lost and found, and more. Followed by *Sarah's Quilt* (2005) and *The Star Garden* (2007).

American Beauty

Lighthearted, fun tales set in the world of beauty, from hair salons to pageants, models to magazines.

Baird-Murray, Kathleen

Face Value: A Novel. 2008. Berkley. ISBN 0425221458. 323p.

Kate is a reporter for a small-town newspaper in England when out of the blue, she is offered the position of beauty editor of an American magazine, which is really strange, considering she is not known as fashionable to any degree. She moves to New York City and is soon swept away by the world of fashion, and quickly begins to learn the business of beauty. When she is sent on assignment to cover plastic surgery in Los Angeles, however, it proves to be more than she can handle and she plans on writing an exposé instead of a positive fluff piece. After all, beauty is more than skin deep.

Brandt, Beverly

The Tiara Club. 2005. St. Martin's Griffin. ISBN 0312341229. 368p.

Second-generation beauty queen Georgia joins her friends, all veterans of the beauty pageant circuit, to come to the aid of Sierra, who is vying for the coveted Shrimp Queen crown. They don't quite know what to make of Sierra, a Yankee who's never taped her breasts up or glued a bathing suit to her bottom to wow the judges. They also wouldn't know what to make of Georgia's secret—she's the inventor of a kitchen gadget that is sold on infomercials. A light and entertaining read.

Cook, Claire

Summer Blowout. 2008. Hyperion. ISBN 1401322417. 256p.

Bella works at her father's chain of beauty salons as a makeup artist. Problem is, so does the rest of her large extended family, including ex-wives, stepmothers, and half-siblings. It wouldn't be so bad, but they are all in each other's business, which drives Bella mad. Family tensions only get worse when Bella discovers that her ex-husband has been dating her younger half-sister and they plan to wed. What happened to her biggest worry being finding the perfect shade of lipstick (all chronicled here)? Many laugh-out-loud scenes and quirky characters make up this fun, breezy read.

Flynn-Hui, Kathleen
⇨ *Beyond the Blonde.* 2005. Warner. ISBN 0446500178. 277p.

Georgia leaves her small-town New Hampshire life far behind her to move to Manhattan and become a colorist at a high-end salon. She manages to hang on to her down-to-earth and likeable charm even though she's working with divas of both the client and coworker varieties. Flynn-Hui, an industry insider, takes no prisoners in this novel, thought to be a thinly veiled exposé of the famous Frederic Fekkai hair empire in New York.

Hazelwood, Robin
Model Student: A Tale of Co-Eds and Cover Girls. 2006. Crown. ISBN 0307337189. 400p.

Emily, a student at Columbia University, tries to balance life as a college student and her dream of being a couture model. However, she soon learns that it's hard to juggle the books and the bronzer at the same time. Leaving for a photo shoot in the Caribbean right before finals week is not the best way to get your grades up, to boot. Former model Hazelwood's novel is just right for fans of *America's Next Top Model.*

Kauffman, Donna
The Cinderella Rules. 2004. Bantam. ISBN 0553382349. 432p.

Darby left her wealthy family to run a ranch in Montana, where she can just be her unpretentious and decidedly unfashionable self. When her younger sister recruits her to play hostess to one of their father's wealthy clients, she finds herself at The Glass Slipper spa for a total makeover by their famous "Glamour Nazis." When she keeps running across the same handsome young man over and over again, will he still be interested when she turns back into her old, comfortably non-glamorous self?

LeClaire, Anne D.
Leaving Eden. 2002. Ballantine. ISBN 0345445740. 293p.

In this charming coming-of-age story, teenage Tallie decides that a make-over is what she needs to enable her to get out of her small town and catapult her to stardom. When The Klip 'n Kurl, the local beauty salon she works at, the of-fers a "Glamour Day," she leaps at the chance to change her appearance, but soon realizes nothing will change the fact that she misses her mother, who had the same dreams of getting out of rural Virginia and living the glittering Hollywood lifestyle. Sweetly told with eccentric characters and heartbreaking moments.

Neale, Naomi
The Mile-High Hair Club. 2005. Making It. ISBN 0843955643. 369p.

Glamorous New Yorker Bailey returns to her hometown in rural Virginia, intending on a short visit with her mother. However, the town is taken over by local beauty queen wannabes, eager to be primed for pageantry by Bailey's aunts, Bits and Bubble. Before she knows what's hit her, Bailey finds herself helping her wacky aunts, and befriends a rebellious young woman determined to become the Butter Bean Queen.

Rendahl, Eileen
Do Me, Do My Roots. 2004. Downtown Press. ISBN 0743471148. 299p.

Emily, Leah, and Claudia are sisters who regularly get together to color each other's hair. But even better than the highlights are the conversations the sisters share, bonding and helping each other through life's challenges. Emily is a young widow caring for her small daughter, Leah is trying to find her Mr. Right but keeps falling for younger men unwilling to commit, and Claudia dates one bad guy after another. The sister's monthly hair-color-and-gossip sessions are interrupted by their father's heart attack, and they realize there are worse things to weather than a little gray hair.

Chapter Four

Mood

Mood as an appeal factor is hard to capture in women's fiction. On the surface, a book may seem laugh-out-loud funny, or it may be a weeper. What's difficult to define is whether the particular mood of a book is its main appeal. Perhaps the plot is what really draws the reader in, not the mood. Readers bring their own moods and perceptions into reading, and what's hysterical to one person might not be funny at all to another.

Tone is the voice of the novel, created by the author by the way she tells the story and the desired effect on the reader. Humor, sadness, gentleness are different tones, and they all serve to create a certain mood for the book.

Something interesting to note is that mood and tone can be of decidedly different appeal to different readers—some readers choose or enjoy a book to match the current mood they are in, while others choose or enjoy a book based on a mood they would like to be in.

The books listed in this chapter all have some mood/tone connection—their main objective is to make the reader laugh, or cry, or feel romantic. The writing styles may be different within each list, but the desired effect is the same. Issue-driven fiction also makes its appearance here because the tone of these titles is decidedly serious.

Cry Me a River

Sometimes all you need is a good weep session. These novels open the tear ducts.

Berg, Elizabeth
Talk Before Sleep. 1994. Random House. ISBN 067943299X. 210p.

Reserved Ann and gregarious Ruth are unlikely best friends. When Ruth is diagnosed with breast cancer, Ann, a former nurse, throws herself into caring for her friend. Ravaged by the disease as the cancer spreads to her brain and lungs, Ruth depends on Ann's skills and her unwavering friendship.

Dart, Iris Rainer
Beaches. 1985. Bantam. Reissue, 2004, Harper Paperbacks. ISBN 0060594772. 204p.

Cee Cee and Bertie meet on a beach in Atlantic City when they are 10 years old; and the novel follows them through 30 years of friendship. They couldn't be more different—Cee Cee is gregarious, brash, and destined to be a star; while Bertie is cautious and quiet. They bring out the best in each other, however, and when Bertie is dying of cancer, Cee Cee drops everything to be by her side. Saw the movie? Now read the book for even more insight into the characters—but be sure to have the tissues handy.

Delinsky, Barbara
Three Wishes. 1997. Simon & Schuster. ISBN 0684845075. 302p.

Bree gets a second chance at life after being hit by a car and pronounced dead at the hospital. A bright light and a voice telling her she will be granted three wishes whisks her back into the world. Her wishes are: fall in love, find her birth mother, and have a child. What happens after her wishes are granted, though? A tear-jerker of the weepiest kind.

Fielding, Joy
⇨ *The First Time.* 2000. Pocket. ISBN 9780743407052. 352p.

The façade of Mattie Hart's seemingly perfect life crumbles around her when her husband leaves her for another woman. She's not too surprised, as she's been ignoring his infidelities for a long time. But this couldn't have come at a worse time—Mattie's just been diagnosed with ALS (Lou Gehrig's Disease), so her guilt-ridden husband comes back to care for her. Although it's a sad and touching story, Fielding manages to keep it from being maudlin.

Hannah, Kristin
On Mystic Lake. 1999. Crown. ISBN 0609602497. 323p.

Annie is ready for the pain of empty-nest syndrome when her beloved daughter leaves for college. She's not prepared for her husband to announce he's leaving her on the same day. Annie heads back to her hometown of Mystic, Washington, to live with her aging dad. But tragedy follows her, from the loss of her childhood best friend to a scary and unexpected premature birth. Bust out the economy-sized box of tissues for this one.

Mitchard, Jacquelyn
Deep End of the Ocean. 1996. Viking. ISBN 9780670865796. 434p.

Beth Cappadora spends nine years searching for her son Ben, who was abducted when he was a toddler. Endless guilt leads her to neglect her other two children and the family tension increases as older son Vincent becomes more and more aggressive at school and at home. When Ben finally returns, it causes more pressure than relief on the beleaguered family.

Noble, Elizabeth
Things I Want My Daughters to Know. 2008. William Morrow. ISBN 9780061122194. 384p.

> Four sisters deal with the death of their beloved mother in this tearjerker. Barbara has written letters to her daughters, ages 15 to 38, and left them behind for the girls to read after she succumbs to cancer. Each daughter has a personal problem to overcome, and Mom's words of wisdom guide the girls through a difficult year.

Rice, Luanne
Cloud Nine. 1999. Bantam. ISBN 0553110632. 323p.

> Sarah Talbot has recovered from a brain tumor. When an emotionally fragile man and his teenage daughter come in to her life, she recognizes the need for family connections and reaches out to her father and her estranged son. Rice's novels often center on the power of love and family, and this emotional tale is a standout.

I Still Miss My Ex, But My Aim Is Getting Better

Revenge stories of all kinds—best served cold, laugh-out-loud funny, or steamy hot.

Andrews, Mary Kay
⇨ *Savannah Breeze.* 2006. HarperCollins. ISBN 0060564660. 448p.

> Bebe Loudermilk loses everything when her con-man boyfriend Reddy disappears after stealing her money, her business, and her home. All she's left with is the Breeze Inn, a rundown motel in a quirky tourist town. When Reddy resurfaces, Bebe gets her best friend, her motel manager, and her eccentric grandfather involved in a kooky grand scheme to fleece him out of what's rightfully hers.

Barrett, Jo
This Is How it Happened: Not a Love Story. 2008. Avon. ISBN 9780061241109. 320p.

> When Madeline is dumped by her boyfriend Carlton, he not only breaks her heart but fires her from the organic food company they started together as well. Furious, she dreams up elaborate revenge schemes, from poisoned brownies to witchcraft. When these prove unsuccessful, she hires a Mafia hit man. Black humor and quirky characters abound.

Goldsmith, Olivia
The First Wives Club. 1992. Poseidon Press. Reprint, 2008, Pocket. ISBN 9781416562832. 576p.

Annie, Brenda, and Elise find themselves dumped for younger models after they have helped their husbands achieve success. When another friend commits suicide after her divorce, the three band together to form the First Wives Club, set on helping each other get revenge and to see justice for their late friend. Juicy and fun.

Medoff, Jill
Good Girls Gone Bad. 2002. William Morrow. ISBN 0066212693. 304p.

When Janey Fabre finally realizes that obsessing about her ex-boyfriend is getting her nowhere, she decides to go to group therapy. The other women she becomes friends with all have their own problems—Valentine has an eating disorder, Laura has a problem with commitment, and Natasha has OCD. Group therapy is not quite what Janey was expecting though—instead of helping her get over the cheating rogue, they help her hatch a revenge plot, which turns deadly by mistake.

Michaels, Fern
The Marriage Game. 2007. Pocket. ISBN 9780743477451. 290p.

Samantha Rainford gets home from her honeymoon to discover she's already been served with divorce papers. But if that's not bad enough, she also finds out there are three other Mrs. Rainfords out there. With the help of her best friend Slick, she joins the other ex-wives in a scheme to get their revenge—even going as far as to enroll in a top-secret private special-ops training camp. Michaels also has a series of books, *Revenge of the Sisterhood,* featuring more action and suspense.

Smith, Haywood
Red Hat Club. 2003. St. Martin's. ISBN 0312316933. 306p.

Southern queens and lifelong friends Diane, Georgia, Linda, SuSu, and Teeny band together for revenge when they suspect Diane's husband of cheating on her. Not only is he cheating on her, he's hiding money and property, and they have the paper trail and computer files to prove it. Surrounding the intrigue is a tale of five women looking back at their lives and looking forward to many shared adventures to come.

Mysterious Ladies

Not quite frothy enough to be just chick lit, not quite meaty enough to satisfy the typical mystery fan, here are novels that have a mystery at the heart of the story, but keep the tone lighthearted and fun.

Anderson, Sheryl J.
Killer Heels. 2004. St. Martin's Minotaur. ISBN 0312319460. 311p.

Advice columnist Molly stumbles across the dead body of a her coworker Teddy and decides to play amateur detective. So who's the main suspect? Teddy's wife; the boss he was carrying on with; or the model mistress? When a handsome homicide detective enters the scene, Molly's more determined than ever to be part of the investigation. Fluffy and fun.

Barbieri, Maggie
⇨ *Murder 101.* 2006. St. Martin's Minotaur. ISBN 0312355378. 276p.

English professor Alison can't manage to keep out of trouble. When her stolen car is recovered with the body of one of her students in the trunk, she's at the top of the list of suspects. Meanwhile, she has to bail her ex-husband out of jail and deal with a burgeoning romance with one of the homicide detectives, all while trying to grade final exams. Fun and frothy.

Carrington, Tori
Sofie Metropolis. **Sofie Metropolis Mysteries.** 2005. Forge. ISBN 0765312409. 288p.

Tired of waitressing and fed up with her cheating boyfriend, Sofie decides it's time for something new. She embarks on a career as a private investigator, but quickly gets bored with missing pet cases. Drama is just around the corner, however, when her cases start to involve cheating spouses, mystery men, and the FBI. Wacky characters and funny situations abound. Followed by *Dirty Laundry* (2006) and *Foul Play* (2007).

Drake, Abby
Good Little Wives. 2007. Avon. ISBN 9780061232213. 304p.

The desperate housewives of New Falls, New York, are shocked when one of their group is charged with the murder of her ex-husband. Shocking, perhaps, but not surprising, since after all, the accused was dumped for a much younger trophy wife. Despite literally being caught with the smoking gun, Kitty claims innocence, and her friend Dana decides to get to the bottom of the case. Campy and fun.

Harris, Lynn
Death By Chick Lit. 2007. Berkley. ISBN 0425215245. 256p.

Lola, an unsuccessful author, is on the case when fellow writer Mimi is found dead in true chick lit style—her throat was slit with a shard from a broken martini glass. Lola hopes that if she unmasks the killer, it could lead to a new book deal and some publicity. Suspects range from the geeky guy who stalks chick lit author signings to Mimi's boyfriend. And then of course, there's Wilma, the founder of the Jane Austen Liberation Front. Would she be on a killing spree, getting rid of low-brow writers? Dark yet funny.

Kandel, Susan
I Dreamed I Married Perry Mason. **Cece Caruso Mysteries.** 2004. William Morrow. ISBN 0060581050. 280p.

Cece, a writer in Los Angeles, is busy researching a book about Earl Stanley Gardner when she finds herself caught up in a decades-old murder case—and a new one. The former beauty queen, distracted by her vintage clothing collection and worries about her daughter, manages to get in hot water the deeper she gets into the unsolved case. Followed by *Not a Girl Detective* (2005), *Shamus in the Green Room* (2006), and *Christietown* (2007).

Sturman, Jennifer
The Pact. **Rachel Benjamin Mysteries.** 2004. Red Dress Ink. ISBN 0373250797. 304p.

Five college friends gather for a wedding, and the groom is murdered after the rehearsal. No one's really sad because he was pretty slimy. The problem comes in when the detectives arrive to investigate and discover almost everyone in attendance had a motive—especially, the five gal pals, who've had a pact since college that they would use whatever means necessary to rescue one another from a bad relationship. So who did it? A fun and breezy chick lit mystery, followed by *The Jinx* (2005) and *The Key* (2006).

Gentle Reads

When all you want is a nice, soft story, these books will fit the bill. The problems are solvable, and the love tends to be chaste, making these a good choice for all ages as well.

Barclay, Tessa
Ties of Affection. 2008. Severn House. ISBN 0727866540. 250p.

Olivia Fletcher runs an eco-friendly housecleaning firm in Surrey, England. When none of her employees are willing to clean the Moorfield family's Victorian, Olivia is left to the task and discovers why—they are unlikable and demanding. Olivia decides to help them all clean up their personal lives as well as their home, and finds herself becoming emotionally attached to the family.

Binchy, Maeve
Evening Class. 1997. Delacorte. ISBN 0385318073. 420p.

Eight Dubliners meet for Italian lessons, and learn life lessons as well. Aidan agrees to co-teach an Italian class in Dublin after being passed over for the headmaster job at his school. Nora is the other teacher, freshly returned to Ireland after the death of her married boyfriend in Sicily. The students range from a bank clerk in need of some self-esteem to a hotel porter with a childlike innocence. Once again, Binchy's irresistible cast of characters shines in this charming novel.

Moyes, Jojo
Windfallen. 2003. William Morrow. ISBN 0060012900. 400p.

Arcadia House is an art deco–era mansion in Merham, a quiet seaside town in southeast England. When a group of bohemians take over the property in the 1950s, the stuffy residents of Merham are not amused, with the exception of teenagers Lottie and Celia, who are delighted with the artistic and unusual new inhabitants. The novel then jumps to the present day to follow Daisy, who is renovating the home as a tourist attraction and upscale hotel. She makes discoveries that lead to Lottie, and the two women become unlikely friends.

Pichler, Rosamunde
➾ *Winter Solstice.* 2000. St. Martin's. ISBN 0312244266. 464p.

Elfrida Phipps retires from a stage career to Cregan, Scotland, with her musician friend Oscar, who has recently lost his wife and daughter in a car crash. They are soon joined by Elfrida's young cousin, Carrie, who is getting over a broken heart, and Carrie's teenage daughter. When a handsome stranger stops by for Christmas, he is of course welcomed into the motley group with open arms. Pilcher creates memorable characters and comforting places in her novels.

Shaw, Rebecca
A Country Affair. **Barleybridge Novels.** 2006. Three Rivers Press. ISBN 9781400098200. 288p.

In this first installment of the Barleybridge trilogy, Kate takes a receptionist job at a veterinary practice in the small English farming village of Barleybridge after failing grades keep her out of vet school. There she meets a rollicking cast of characters, from eccentric pet owners to the warm-hearted staff. Followed by *Country Wives* (2006) and *Country Lovers* (2007).

Willett, Marcia
A Week in Winter. 2002. St. Martin's. ISBN 0312287852. 342p.

Widow Maud wants to sell her Cornwall estate, Moorgate, and retire to Devon. But she can't choose among the potential buyers. There's her stepdaughter Selina, who after 30 years still hasn't forgiven Maud for marrying her father; the building contractor who has restored the home; and a young woman with a secret. Romances and family secrets come to light, complicating matters.

Wingate, Lisa
Tending Roses. 2001. New American Library. ISBN 0451203070. 274p.

Katie moves to her grandmother's farm with her husband and baby son, with the unpleasant task of convincing Grandma Rose to move from her beloved homestead to a nursing home. Katie discovers Rose's diary, full of stories celebrating the power of love and the importance of family, and she soon realizes just how important her grandmother (and the farm) is to her.

Beyond Oprah

When you're in the mood for something introspective, try one of these. Also known as problem novels, or issue-driven novels, these books explore the darker side of life and how women cope with personal tragedies.

Hegland, Jean
⇨ *Windfalls.* 2004. Pocket. ISBN 0743470079. 339p.

This powerful look at motherhood and poverty follows the parallel lives of Anna and Cerise, two very different women. The story opens as the two young women learn they are pregnant, and follows them through a single choice—whether to keep the baby. Anna ends up married with two children but unhappy—she's abandoned her passion for art. Cerise, an unwed mother of two, struggles with poverty and ends up homeless. Ultimately, their two stories quietly merge.

Johnson, Rebecca
And Sometimes Why. 2008. Putnam. ISBN 9780399154522. 320p.

A tragedy causes family upheaval. Sixteen-year-old Helen lies in a coma after a car accident, and everyone involved gets a story here. Her father Darius refuses to believe she won't recover, while her mother Sophia becomes obsessed with Helen's secret boyfriend, Bobby, who also died in the crash. Their other daughter, Miranda, withdraws from the family; and Harry, the driver of the other vehicle, allows his life to be consumed by guilt, even though he was not at fault—Bobby was driving drunk with an impaired motorcycle. An interesting look into different lives touched by the same incident.

Larsen, Judy Merrill
All the Numbers: A Novel. 2006. Ballantine. ISBN 034548536X. 304p.

Ellen is a divorced working mother of two boys, living a fairly mundane life, when tragedy strikes. Her 11-year-old son James is accidentally hit by a teenager on a Jet Ski, and dies from head injuries. Ellen must overcome her grief to seek justice for her son and to mend her family's wounds. Can she find forgiveness and move on?

McDonough, Yona Zeldis
In Dahlia's Wake. 2005. Doubleday. ISBN 0385503628. 293p.

Naomi and Rick are a Brooklyn couple struggling in the aftermath of their young daughter's death. Rick was driving with Dahlia in the backseat when what could have been just a minor fender-bender results in her death. Unable to forgive her husband, Naomi rejects Rick and throws herself into volunteer work. Rick, meanwhile, deals with this rejection by having an affair with a coworker. A sensitive portrayal of a marriage torn apart by grief.

Miller, Sue

Lost in the Forest. 2005. Knopf. ISBN 1400042267. 256p.

After leaving her first husband, Mark, for cheating on her, Eva is happily remarried. When her second husband dies in a tragic accident, she is devastated and finds she can't cope with her three children, two daughters from her first marriage and a son from her second. Mark reappears in her life to help out, and finds that he's still in love with her. Meanwhile, their younger and emotionally unsure daughter finds herself lured into a dangerous relationship with an older man. What will become of this fractured family?

Picoult, Jodi

Perfect Match. 2002. Pocket. ISBN 0743418727. 350p.

Known for her hard-hitting and timely family dramas, Picoult delivers plenty of blows in this one. Nina, a district attorney, knows how hard it is to prosecute sex crimes when the victims are juvenile. When her young son Nathaniel is molested and identifies their priest as the perpetrator, Nina becomes frustrated by the threat of an unsatisfactory outcome, and takes the law into her own hands, shooting the priest at his arraignment. During her own trial, DNA evidence shows a shocking fact—the priest may have been innocent. Twists and turns abound.

Quindlen, Anna

One True Thing. 1994. Random House. ISBN 067940712X. 289p.

Ellen abandons a promising career in journalism to return home and care for her mother, Kate, who is dying of cancer. Through long hours as her mother's companion, Ellen must deal with Kate's pain and suffering, her father's coldness, and family secrets. When Kate dies of a morphine overdose, Ellen is unjustly arrested for homicide. A fascinating look at a number of issues—dysfunctional families, the euthanasia debate, dealing with a loved one's terminal illness—all wrapped up in a young woman's search for self.

Rice, Luanne

Perfect Summer. 2003. Bantam. ISBN 0553584049. 429p.

Bay McCabe has a seemingly perfect life—a successful banker husband and three beautiful children—but one day, her life is shattered. Her husband Sean goes missing and shortly after, the FBI shows up to tell her that he is under investigation for embezzlement. Suddenly, Bay and her children are hunted by the press, shunned by their community, and completely broke. Things only look worse when Sean's body is found and rumors of an affair surface.

Robinson, Roxana

Cost. 2008. Farrar, Straus & Giroux. ISBN 0374271879. 432p.

Julia, an art professor, is spending the summer in Maine with her domineering elderly father and her mother, who is suffering from Alzheimer's.

When she discovers her youngest son Jack is addicted to heroin, she calls upon older son, her ex-husband, and her sister for help, and the family decides on a tough intervention. A heartbreaking and no-holds-barred look at a family dealing with addiction.

Shreve, Anita

Strange Fits of Passion. 1991. Harcourt Brace Jovanovich. Reprint, 2005, Harvest Books. ISBN 0156031396. 342p.

Maureen and her baby daughter fled New York City on the run from her abusive husband, a prominent and respected journalist. When he finds her in a small Maine coastal town, she resorts to deadly violence. Almost 20 years later, the past catches up with her as a reporter finds her again to try and atone for her sensational coverage of the event.

Swick, Marly

Evening News. 1999. Little, Brown. ISBN 0316825336. 356p.

Giselle goes into shock after her nine-year-old son Teddy accidentally shoots his two-year-old half-sister while playing with a gun. Giselle's husband Dan, Teddy's stepfather, is unable forgive him; but in spite of her own grief, Giselle cannot blame her young son. The situation threatens to tear the couple apart.

Ladies Who Laugh

When you need a pick-me-up, nothing beats being able to laugh out loud with a good book. These authors are known for funny characters, situations, and dialogue.

Ballis, Stacey

⇨ *Room for Improvement.* 2006. Berkley. ISBN 9780425209820. 304p.

Chicago interior designer Lily takes a job with *Swap/Meet,* a reality TV show that pairs up singles looking for a new room and a new love interest. She thinks it's going to be simple and fun, but dealing with a half-wit host, crazy contestants, a cranky but cute carpenter, and a diva designer makes things difficult. When a playboy producer gets into the mix (and into Lily's bed), life becomes even more complicated. Light and funny, with snappy dialogue and crazy situations.

Carter, Mary

Accidentally Engaged. 2007. Kensington. ISBN 0758215398. 304p.

Clair, a fortune-teller, has just told Rachel that she'll end up in a bad marriage. Surprisingly, that's what Rachel wanted to hear, so she leaves behind her three-carat engagement ring and tells Clair to return it to Jake, a wealthy winery owner. When Clair shows up at what was supposed to be Rachel and

Jake's engagement party, she finds herself impersonating the bride-to-be to please Jake's extended family and a group of investors. Wackiness ensues as Clair falls for the best man.

Holden, Wendy
Simply Divine. 1999. Plume. ISBN 0452281679. 291p.

Londoner Jane Bentley, a magazine writer, finds herself ghostwriting a column detailing the exploits of celebrity socialite Champagne D'Vyne. Champagne is beautiful but ridiculously stupid, and Jane has a heck of a time keeping her under control while trying to manage her own life, which includes being dumped by her boyfriend and trying to help out a friend in need. Witty puns and high satire along with over-the-top characters will keep you laughing.

Kinsella, Sophie
The Undomestic Goddess. 2005. Dial Press. ISBN 9780385338684. 384p.

Samantha Sweeting is an overworked, overstressed lawyer. After she makes a mistake at work that will cost her her career, she has a breakdown, gets on the first train to anywhere, and finds herself in the country. Looking for assistance to get back home, she knocks on the door of a manor house only to be mistaken for a hired housekeeper. She decides to go along with the charade, figuring the job can't be any worse than the law firm... only she doesn't know how to clean or cook. Absolutely hysterical.

Markham, Wendy
Slightly Single. Red Dress Ink. 2002. ISBN 0373250134. 288p.

When her loser actor boyfriend leaves for summer stock, insecure New Yorker Tracey decides to perform a makeover on all aspects of her life. She gets a new job, loses weight, finds a better apartment, and meets a new man— but she's just interested in being friends. Tracey's witty, sarcastic sense of humor makes her a fun heroine to keep company with. Followed by *Slightly Settled* (2004) and *Slightly Engaged* (2006).

Mason, Sarah
Party Girl. 2005. Ballantine. ISBN 0345469569. 336p.

Party planner Isabel has been given the chance to throw a circus-themed charity ball for 500 guests at a country estate. This could be a career coup, but there are a host of problems—she has only one month to prepare, she's got personal problems (her boyfriend has just dumped her), and the host of the party is her childhood nemesis, Simon. As they begin to work together, they can't deny their attraction for one another, even as everything that could go wrong does—hysterically.

Naylor, Claire
Dog Handling. 2002. Ballantine. ISBN 0345453387. 342p.

Liv isn't really sure she wants to get married, but she's still shocked when her boyfriend calls off the wedding. She flees to Australia, where she embarks on a new life, a new career (selling bras at a flea market!) and makes new friends. Two of them, zany gay men addicted to *The Rules,* decide that to land and keep a new man, she needs to learn the art of dog handling—treating them as though they are pets that need to be tamed.

The Thrill of It All

Romantic suspense is a catchall term, and the books get lumped in either the romance or the mystery genre. Instead of just focusing on a romantic or mysterious element, these books deliver strong women characters with fully developed backstories.

Adler, Elizabeth
Sailing to Capri. 2006. St. Martin's. ISBN 0312339658. 371p.

When her beloved boss is murdered, Daisy Keene is shocked; but it seems he was suspicious of his enemies, and had even hired investigator Harry Montana prior to his death. Harry's got instructions to assemble the suspects on a cruise ship for the reading of the will and to ferret out the killer. Naturally attracted to each other, Daisy and Harry are also distracted by the cast of characters. Armchair travel, light suspense, and good characters are hallmarks of Adler's writing.

Allen, Charlotte Vale
Grace Notes. 2002. Mira. ISBN 1551669064. 234p.

Successful author Grace is accustomed to being e-mailed by readers seeking advice. Her novels focus on women in abusive relationships, so she doesn't blink an eye when she finds herself involved with a reader, Stephanie, who is being abused by her husband—or so she claims. When Stephanie murders her husband, Grace finds herself in dangerously deep waters. Twists and turns abound.

Brundage Elizabeth
The Doctor's Wife. 2004. Viking. ISBN 0670033162. 342p.

Two couples come together in love and violence. Enigmatic Lydia is married to Simon, who is having an affair with gregarious Annie, who is married to Michael, a doctor who is being targeted by the anti-abortion group that Lydia is in. Twisted and complex, this story draws the reader in with a thrilling premise, but keeps the reader involved through the intricate relationships of the characters and the choices they make.

Diamond, Diana
The Good Sister. 2002. St. Martin's. ISBN 0312291655. 296p.

Two sisters inherit a billion-dollar business, and soon find their relationship challenged by a suspicious suitor. Although glamorous Catherine and plain Jennifer are very different, they are well suited to run the giant communications company their father left them—Catherine has marketing savvy while Jennifer is a techno-genius. When Jennifer is seduced by a handsome actor, Catherine grows wary and soon attempts are made on both sisters' lives—but by whom?

French, Nicci
Catch Me When I Fall. 2006. Grand Central. ISBN 0446578487. 336p.
Bipolar Holly has a loving husband and great friends, but she continuously makes reckless mistakes that result in her being stalked and blackmailed. Her family and friends try to save her, but she can't seem to break free of her manic episodes, from having sex with strangers to gambling away thousands. As those closest begin to abandon her, when she needs them the most—someone is trying to kill her.

Howard, Linda
⇨ *Open Season.* 2001. Pocket. ISBN 0671034421. 310p.
When librarian Daisy turns 34, she decides it's time to shed her stereotypical image. She undergoes a makeover, which boosts her confidence, and decides to enter the dating world. Unfortunately, she catches the eye of a murderer. Daisy is a wonderful character in search of who she really wants to be. Suspenseful, steamy, and laugh-out-loud funny all at the same time.

Parsons, Julie
Eager to Please. 2000. Simon & Schuster. ISBN 0743219317. 303p.
Rachel has served 12 years in an Irish prison for the murder of her husband, a crime that her brother-in-law actually committed. Given temporary release, she hatches a plan of revenge. She also tries to reach out to her estranged teenage daughter, who does not believe that Rachel is innocent. Well-written and compelling.

Beautiful and Blessed Are They: Christian Chick Lit

Not all chick lit is sex, shopping, and shoes. These gentler Christian tales possess the same spunk as their secular counterparts, but feature religious young women and manage to slip some mild evangelism into their stories.

Carlson, Melody
These Boots Weren't Made for Walking. 2007. Waterbrook Press. ISBN 9781400073139. 320p.
Cassidy claims to be an old-fashioned girl, but she's just as obsessed by shoes and romance as any other chick lit heroine. When her boyfriend dumps

her for a new woman he meets at church and she loses her job in the same week, Cassie flees to her hometown for some comfort. Unfortunately, it's not to be found at home, since her mother has had a makeover and is enjoying a new thriving social life. Cassie decides to embark on her own life makeover and reinvents herself. Lighthearted, funny, and frothy.

Dayton, Anne, and May Vanderbilt

Consider Lily. 2006. Broadway Books. ISBN 9780385518307. 382p.

Still living with her parents at age 27, devout Lily decides on a major life makeover. She trades her sports gear and jeans for flirting lessons and fishnet stockings. Then she starts writing an anonymous blog called Fashion Victim that gets picked up by the *San Francisco Weekly,* but she becomes troubled when her editor spices up her columns without her permission. She also has difficulty deciding if her new boyfriend is true. Good-girl chick lit.

Hauck, Rachel

Love Starts With Elle. 2008. Thomas Nelson. ISBN 1595543384. 320p.

Elle, the owner of a successful art gallery in South Carolina, has a great life. She loves her small-town life and her career, and she has great friends, so what more could she ask for? When a handsome pastor named Jeremiah sweeps her off her feet, she's ready to accept his proposal—that is, until Jeremiah is transferred to a congregation in a Dallas. Is she ready to move away from all she loves for the man she loves?

Leigh, Tamara

⇨ *Splitting Harriet.* 2007. Multnomah Books. ISBN 9781590529287. 400p.

Preacher's daughter Harriet, a former wild child, decides to go the straight and narrow. She keeps busy juggling her part-time jobs as a women's ministry director and a waitress at a local café. When her church hires a cute consultant to spice up the services, Harriet worries about sliding back to her party girl past. Romance author Leigh has several other similar Christian chick lit titles, including *Stealing Adda* (2005) and *Perfecting Kate* (2007).

Meissner, Susan

Blue Heart Blessed. 2008. Harvest House. ISBN 0736919171. 288p.

When Daisy is left at the altar, she makes lemonade out of lemons by opening a secondhand bridal gown shop, figuring that doomed wedding dresses deserve a second chance at love. Each gown has a tiny blue heart sewn into the seams that has been blessed by Daisy's friend, Father Laurent. When the elderly Episcopal pastor falls ill, his son Ramsey comes to take him away, much to Daisy's chagrin. Even though she fights with Ramsey, she can't stop thinking about him—can she let herself have a second chance at love as well?

Walker, Laura Jensen
Miss Invisible. 2007. Thomas Nelson. ISBN 1595540687. 320p.

Professional cake baker Freddie lets her plus size dampen her self-esteem, making her a doormat at work and a wallflower on the social scene. When her outspoken new friend Deborah encourages her to come out of her shell, Freddie feels as though God has put Deborah in her life for a reason, and realizes it's time to be the best she can be. A charming heroine and a well-told story of a wallflower just waiting for encouragement.

Paranormal Paramours

A recent trend in romance and women's fiction has been quirky paranormal tales. These selections feature well-rounded characters in addition to the out-there atmospheres.

Davidson, MaryJanice
Unwed and Undead. **Undead Novels.** 2004. Berkley Sensation. ISBN 042519485X. 277p.

First in the Undead series, former model Betsy Taylor comes back to life after being killed in a car accident—and realizes that she is a vampire, and not just any old vampire, but queen of the vampires. Being the queen of vampires allows Betsy certain niceties such as the ability to venture out in the daytime, a good perk. Hilarious.

Hallaway, Tate
Tall, Dark & Dead. 2006. Berkley Books. ISBN 0425209725. 304p.

Garnet gives up witchcraft to manage an occult bookstore in Madison, Wisconsin. Tired of being chased by witch-slaying Vatican agents, she gives up her powers. When Sebastian Von Traum patronizes the store, she immediately realizes he's a vampire/warlock; and when she discovers the agents are after him as well, the two team up. Now she's back in the game. Very supernatural and lots of fun. Followed by *Dead Sexy* (2007) and *Romancing the Dead* (2008).

Kenner, Julie
Carpe Demon: Adventures of a Demon-Hunting Soccer Mom. 2005. Berkley Books. ISBN 0425202526. 368p.

Kate Connor works as a demon hunter, à la Buffy the Vampire Slayer. She's been out of commission for the past few years though to raise a family. When a murderous demon invades her home life, Kate's back in action. Can she manage to fight off evil and still get the kids to Gymboree on time? And will she be able to keep her past a secret? Very fun, with plenty of action. Followed by *California Demon* (2006) and *Demons Are Forever* (2007).

Klasky, Mindy
⇨*The Girl's Guide to Witchcraft.* 2006. Red Dress Ink. ISBN 0373896077. 432p.

Librarian Jane Madison discovers a hidden witchcraft room in her home, and realizes she's got a talent for spells. A handsome Warder appears to guide her along the way, and she begins to have lots of fun creating romance for herself, helping out her struggling library, and figuring out just where she wants her life to head. Utterly charming chick lit with a believable supernatural twist. Followed by *Sorcery and the Single Girl* (2007).

McInnis, Sheri
Devil May Care. 2003. Atria. ISBN 0743464842. 376p.

Aspiring New York City actress Sally gets a streak of good luck after meeting the head of a television network. He's rich, attractive, and they begin a romance—with one problem. He's Satan. Literally, not just a bad guy, but the Prince of Darkness. As her career skyrockets, can Sally ignore the dead rivals piling up, or is it time to write the Dear Lucifer letter? Wicked, wicked fun.

McKelden, Shannon
Venus Envy. 2006. Forge. ISBN 0765315858. 336p.

After a string of bad boyfriends, Rachel swears off love for good. Enter the Greek goddess Venus, who's been banished to Earth by Zeus and forced to play matchmaker for lonely young women. Venus is the ultimate chick lit character—obsessed with romance, shoes, and shopping. Unfortunately Rachel is as steadfast as they come and doesn't go along willingly with Venus' plans. Lighthearted and cute.

Stivers, Valerie
Blood Is the New Black. 2007. Three Rivers Press. ISBN 9780307352132. 320p.

Kate takes a summer job at a fashion magazine and begins to notice some odd things about her new coworkers. Many of them sleep all day, the blinds are always drawn, and there's a no-garlic policy in the lunchroom. And oh, what about the dead bodies popping up all over town? Hysterical, with fully rounded characters.

Isn't It Romantic?

There's a fine line between romance and women's fiction. These contemporary romance novels feature characters who have real depth, and their stories feature more than just love and sex.

Brockway, Connie
Skinny Dipping. 2008. Onyx. ISBN 0451412443. 432p.

Mimi's family wants to sell their summer retreat, and although she doesn't really want to take it over—she shuns any kind of commitment—she doesn't want to see some developer turn the site into a McMansion. When she takes a job caring for the injured young man next door, she finds herself falling in love with his wealthy and successful father, much to her surprise. Queen of the Slackers meets King of the Overachievers. Zany, eccentric characters and fun family dynamics set this apart from the romance pack.

Gibson, Rachel
True Confessions. 2001. Avon. ISBN 0380814382. 384p.

Tabloid reporter (think *Weekly World News*) Hope Spencer is sent to a tiny Idaho town to drum up some alien adventure stories for her editor. She couldn't wait to get out of Los Angeles after a bad divorce and a bout of writer's block, but she's unprepared for the chilly reception she gets from the locals. Sheriff Dan Taber is immediately attracted to her, but needs to keep his distance for the sake of his reputation and his young son. Snappy dialogue and thorough backstories for the characters round out this sweet yet sexy romance.

Kleypas, Lisa
Sugar Daddy. 2007. St. Martin's. ISBN 9780312351625. 384p.

Liberty Jones takes a job as a personal assistant to a wealthy businessman, Churchill, a kindly older man who takes a paternal shine to Liberty and the younger sister she's raising alone. Churchill's son Gage thinks Liberty's a gold digger, and naturally the sparks fly as they get to know one another. When Liberty's childhood sweetheart enters the mix, she's forced to choose between the two. Liberty's family story and the dynamics between all of the characters are the real heart of this romance novel.

Phillips, Susan Elizabeth
⇨*Natural Born Charmer*. 2007. William Morrow. ISBN 9780060734572. 400p.

Blue Bailey discovers her boyfriend has another girlfriend, and she's the odd man out. Stuck with no home and no employment, she meets football player Dean Robillard and tries her hardest to resist his charms. When he offers her a job house-sitting on his Tennessee farm, she figures it's better than nothing. The sexual tension between Blue and Dean is fun, but the real charm of this novel is Dean's eccentric family, made up of his estranged mother; the rock star who may or may not be his father; and the preteen sister he never knew he had who shows up on his doorstep.

Smith, Deborah
The Crossroads Café. 2006. BelleBooks. ISBN 0976876051. 395p.

Glamorous movie star Cathy is horribly disfigured in a paparazzi car chase. She runs away to her hometown in North Carolina, determined to hide from the world. When she meets Thomas, a widower who lost his wife and son on September 11, the two realize they can start over again if they can only trust each other. A sweet romance with heart.

Wiggs, Susan

Summer at Willow Lake. 2006. Mira. ISBN 0778323250. 500p.

Olivia will do anything to save the summer camp that's been in her family for decades, even if it means being nice to Connor, the handyman hired to renovate the camp for her grandparents' 50th wedding anniversary. Turns out Olivia and Connor knew each other at camp, and he broke her heart. Will he do the same years later? Peppered with humorous flashbacks to their summer camp days, this is a charming romance and lovely family story in one.

Turn Up the Heat: Sexy Stories

Similar to the previous list, this list showcases sexy contemporary romances that transcend the genre—the characters and their stories are more developed than an average romance paperback, and they offer a little more spice and sexiness than other women's fiction titles.

Crusie, Jennifer

⇨ *Crazy for You.* 1999. St. Martin's. ISBN 0312198493. 325p.

Quinn is pretty laid back and likes her life to be calm and straightforward, pretty much doing whatever everyone else wants. When her boyfriend decides he doesn't want to keep the stray dog she found and takes it to the pound against her wishes, she realizes she's tired of being a doormat and all hell breaks loose. She dumps the boring boyfriend, gets the dog back, and decides it's time to sleep with Nick, her best friend. Bad-boy Nick provides just what she needs—a fun, lusty romp. Will their sexy fling turn into real love? Cruise has a knack for snappy dialogue and realistic characters that are fun to read about.

Gibson, Rachel

Not Another Bad Date. 2008. Avon. ISBN 0061178047. 384p.

Adele has managed to get far away from her small-town roots in Cedar Creek, Texas. Her college sweetheart, Zach, married someone else, so Adele decided she was better off far far away. When her sister needs her to come home, Adele goes to help, and wouldn't you know it, runs into Zach, who is now divorced, and hunkier than ever. And oh yes, the sexual tension between the two only intensified over the years. An interesting side plot involving Adele's sister's family helps make this a more engrossing read.

Kovetz, Lisa Beth

Tuesday Erotica Club. 2006. Sourcebooks. ISBN 140220664X. 332p.

Bored Aimee starts a literary club at the law firm where she works. When the focus switches from poetry and short stories to erotica, most of the women drop out. The few who remain gather at lunchtime to share their sexy tales, based on their own sexual adventures and fantasies. At the heart of the novel though are four women with distinct personalities and an interesting path to friendship.

Lloyd, Joan Elizabeth
Never Enough. 2003. Kensington. ISBN 0758201095. 274p.

Tracy is fairly conservative, particularly when it comes to love—she got burned by her ex-husband in a bad divorce and vows to never date again. Grudgingly, she agrees to teach her sister's course on intimacy at an upstate New York resort, and realizes it's time to not only lose her inhibitions but to have some sexy fun herself. Luckily for her, the resort manager is a hunk and ready to introduce her to an erotic world of pleasure. Fully developed characters and interesting insights into their personalities move this sexy tale forward, but it's not for those who blush easily.

McCarthy, Erin
Houston, We Have a Problem. 2004. Kensington. ISBN 075820597X. 293p.

Josie is undeniably attracted to Dr. Houston Hayes, who works at the hospital where she's completing her residency, but isn't sure how he feels about her. Every time she gets near him she gets clumsy and can't speak. Oh, but he knows—and is just as attracted to her. Houston decides that the only way they will be able to work together is if they cut the sexual tension by giving in to just one night of passion. Too bad one night isn't enough for either of them! When a career-ending accident threatens to derail him, will Josie stand by his side?

Moore, Kate
Sexy Lexy. 2005. Love Spell/Dorchester. ISBN 0505526239. 352p.

Alexandra, a personal trainer, pens a workout book designed to help couples in the bedroom. It rockets her to fame, which she is utterly unprepared for, so she moves to a small town in the hopes of hiding out and starting a new career, taking over a bed and breakfast. The hunky handyman provides more than his carpentry skills, and all is well—until someone shows up with a copy of her book. Will her notoriety spoil their red-hot romance? Nicely developed characters and funny situations round out this novel.

Chapter Five

Language

Language is a difficult appeal factor to pin down in most genres, and especially for a fluid genre like women's fiction. It is not usually what a reader looks for most in a book of this sort—with women's fiction, the readers wants to know if they'll like the character or the story, not what kind of language or pacing the writer uses.

That said, these lists group together novels based on a common theme of language or writing style—from witty repartee to epistolary fiction. Literary women's fiction is also found here.

Fast Talk

Witty repartee is the hallmark of these novels.

Cabot, Meg
⇨ *Queen of Babble.* 2006. William Morrow. ISBN 0060851988. 320p.

    Lizzie just can't keep her mouth shut, and the consequences are often hilarious. She heads off to London to spend time with her new boyfriend, who turns out to be a liar and a cheat. Determined to cut her losses, she heads to France to hang out with Shari, a friend who is catering weddings at a fancy château. On the train there, she shares her sad story with her handsome seat partner, only to find out he owns the chateau. When she meets his upper-class family, they are less than impressed with her big mouth. This fast-paced, very funny read is followed by *Queen of Babble in the Big City* (2007) and *Queen of Babble Gets Hitched* (2008).

Carroll, Leslie

Herself. 2007. Avon. ISBN 9780060859954. 320p.

Washington, D.C., speechwriter Tessa escapes to Dublin after a personal and professional crisis. When the congressman she works for and dates (never a good mix) becomes embroiled in a scandal, she realizes she was really in love with his political persona, which she helped create and market. Far from home, she meets Jamie, a fisherman who alternately cracks her up and dispenses poetic wisdom. One-liners abound in this upbeat romantic tale.

Crusie, Jennifer

Bet Me. 2004. St. Martin's. ISBN 0312303467. 352p.

Unlikely lovers Min and Cal are determined to not get along, but they just can't help themselves. Min thinks that Cal is only trying to date her because he made a bet with her ex that he could bed her within a month. Cal likes a challenge, of course, but unexpectedly finds himself falling for Min. Crusie's books are usually considered contemporary romance, but her knack for depicting the nuanced relationships between friends and family allows her to sit comfortably in the women's fiction camp. Snappy dialogue between the two main characters makes this a winning bet.

Green, Jane

Straight Talking. 2003. Bantam. ISBN 0767915593. 304p.

TV producer Tasha and her saucy friends navigate the London dating scene. Tasha has a jerk for a boyfriend; Andrea is just one of the guys; Emma has been engaged three times but somehow can't get her current guy to commit; and Mel is stuck in a loveless relationship. Salty language and keen observations make for a very humorous read.

Macpherson, Suzanne

Hysterical Blondeness. 2006. Avon. ISBN 0060775009. 384p.

When Patti signs up for an experimental weight loss program, she gets more than she bargained for. As a side effect of the pills, her mousy brown hair turns platinum blonde, changing everything in her life—blondes do have more fun! She gets promoted at work, and her crush is now interested in her. However, so is her good friend and roommate Paul, who liked her even when she was overweight and not as glamorous. Witty and quick dialogue effortlessly flows between the characters.

Never Hit "Reply All"

It's always fun to read someone else's letters or e-mails. These novels tell their stories through e-mails, phone messages, faxes, and notes.

Ahern, Cecelia
➪ *Rosie Dunne.* 2005. Hyperion. ISBN 140130091X. 256p.

A delightful chronicle of the lives of Rosie and her childhood sweetheart Alex, told through notes, letters, e-mails, and phone calls. Fated to be together, the pair becomes separated when Alex's family moves from Ireland to America during high school. Over the next decade, a series of miscommunications and missed opportunities keep the two on the brink. It's easy to forget you're reading an entire book of letters because Ahern infuses real vitality and lively characters into the story.

Archer, Jennifer
Sandwiched. 2005. Harlequin. ISBN 0373230346. 298p.

Meet recently divorced Cici, her widowed mother Belle, and her teenage daughter, Erin through a mix of letters, e-mails, and instant messages. Cici's bitter and depressed, so vivacious Belle attempts to get her out of the house and into the arms of a new man. Meanwhile, Erin longs to break free from her mother's strict ways and controlling grasp. A delightful family story told in a fresh manner.

Cabot, Meg
Every Boy's Got One. 2005. Avon Trade. ISBN 0060085460. 352p.

A heart, that is. Jane Harris goes to Italy to be the maid of honor in the elopement of her best friends, Holly and Mark. When the Italian government refuses to marry them without a special form, Jane devises a plan to come to the rescue. Toss in a cute but snarky best man, warring in-laws-to-be, and Jane's international fame as a cartoonist, and you get an over-the-top, fun, fluffy tale. The plot unfolds through a series of e-mails, PDA logs, journal entries, and Web site message board entries.

Dyer, Chris
Wanderlust. 2003. Plume. ISBN 0452283795. 273p.

Kate is a globe-trotting travel writer, so naturally her best form of communication is e-mail. She tries to juggle her relationships from afar via the Web, but miscommunication abounds. Her mother, her best friend, and her boss receive daily reports from Kate as well. How does she manage to get her travel column done in between all the e-mailing? Charming and cute.

Efken, Meredith
SAHM I Am. 2005. Steeple Hill Café. ISBN 0373785518. 336p.

This Christian fiction offering is the story five stay-at-home moms (SAHMs). Told entirely in e-mails, Brenna, Dulcie, Jocelyn, Phyllis, and Zelia meet through an e-mail discussion group and form online friendships. When they group's moderator gets on all of their nerves, they decide to form their own chat group, with funny results, as they chat about light topics such as home-schooling and child-rearing, as well as the heavier stuff—infertility, marital difficulties, and chronic illness.

Harte, Kelly
Guilty Feet. 2003. Red Dress Ink. ISBN 0373250266. 314p.

> To teach her boyfriend Dan a lesson, Jo moves out of their flat in Leeds, England. When he doesn't come running after her, she decides to create a new Internet identity for herself and pursue him online, with hysterical results. As Dan opens up to her, she realizes she was wrong, but how will she go about getting him back?

Landvik, Lorna
'Tis the Season!: A Novel. 2008. Ballantine. ISBN 0345499751. 240p.

> Young socialite Caroline Dixon (a Paris Hilton type) gets out of rehab and attempts to live a more stable life. Having alienated everyone she knows by writing a bitter letter that gets leaked to the tabloids, she goes into hiding and tries to reach out to people from her past, including her former nanny and the ranch hand who was kind to her as a teenager. Narrated in a series of letters, e-mails, and gossip-column snippets, this is a quick, charming read.

Newland, Benedicte, and Pascale Smets
And God Created the Au Pair. 2005. Plume. ISBN 0452287286. 370p.

> Two sisters communicate across continents by e-mail in this humorous novel. Nell lives in Toronto and finds herself dealing with her three children as a stay-at-home mom while Charlotte, in London, is lucky enough to have not one but three au pairs. They trade witty horror stories about potty training, seemingly useless husbands, and the never-ending lists of home repairs. Written by two actual sisters.

St. Claire, Rocki
Hit Reply. 2004. Downtown Press. ISBN 0743486242. 352p.

> Amber and her friends chat online about their love lives in this e-mail novel. Married mom Stephanie is flirting online with a former co-worker, while Julie and Amber seek out past flames on the Internet. If you've ever wanted to browse through someone else's e-mail account, this one's for you.

Dear Diary

Even better than sneaking a peek at someone's in-box is getting to read their private journal. These stories unfold through a series of diary entries.

Baer, Judy
The Whitney Chronicles. 2004. Steeple Hill. ISBN 0373785267. 336p.

> Whitney Blake tries to get a handle on her life and relationships by keeping a journal to track her goals of losing weight and finding a man. Once she

starts charting her progress, good things start to happen, including not one but two possible suitors. Charming Evangelical Christian chick lit, followed by *The Baby Chronicles* (2007).

Berg, Elizabeth
Pull of the Moon. 2000. Berkley Trade. ISBN 0425176487. 193p.

Middle-aged Nan's tale of self-discovery is revealed through her diary entries and letters to her husband. She hits the road, leaving behind her marriage and her college-bound daughter, to find where she fits in the world. She makes decisions about her life and chronicles the people and places she encounters on her journey.

Downey, Annie
Hot and Bothered. 2006. Algonquin Books of Chapel Hill. ISBN 156512474X. 304p.

The unnamed narrator of this book is a mother of two in her late 30s, dealing with a rat of a husband who is currently parading his status as a Sex Addicts Anonymous member around town, along with his new girlfriend. She decides it's time to move on, and ends up leaving Cambridge, Massachusetts, for Cape Cod. Very funny and fast paced.

Fielding, Helen
⇨ *Bridget Jones's Diary: A Novel.* 1998. Viking. ISBN 0670880728. 271p.

Ah yes, the book that started the Chick Lit craze. Insecure Bridget smokes too much, eats too much, worries too much, and chronicles it all in her diary. Somehow, she finds herself in the most embarrassing predicaments, from a mix-up at a costume party to exposing her bum on national TV. She also looks for true love. At turns hysterical and touching, this one is sure to hit close to home. Followed by *Bridget Jones: The Edge of Reason* (2000).

Kent, Debra
The Affair. Diary of V series. 2001. Warner. ISBN 0446610496. 305p.

Valerie keeps a journal chronicling the affair she wants to have with Eddie, the man who cares for the plants at her office. She's not usually an adulteress, mind you, but she wants revenge after discovering her husband's infidelities. Uninhibited Valerie tells it like it is. Followed by *The Breakup* (2001) and *Happily Ever After* (2001).

Macomber, Debbie
Between Friends. 2002. Mira Books. ISBN 1551669056. 332p.

Told in diary entries and correspondence, this story follows the 30-year friendship between Jillian and Lesley. Rich girl Jill befriends her poor classmate in grade school, and their relationship remains strong despite the different paths they take. Valedictorian Jill heads off for law school while pregnant Lesley marries an older man.

Oliver, Julia
Devotion: A Novel. 2006. University of Georgia Press. ISBN 082032874X. 206p.

The notebooks and journal entries of the youngest daughter of Confederate president Jefferson Davis are re-created here. Varina Anne, nicknamed Winnie, remembers the South in the years following the Civil War. In the late 19th century, she was known as the official Daughter of the Confederacy, a cultural symbol of the Old South. An early feminist, this was a designation she was not happy with. Romances and family relationships are showcased in this heavily researched novel.

Smith, Lee
On Agate Hill: A Novel. 2006. Algonquin. ISBN 1565124529. 416p.

Tuscany discovers a young girl's diary in the attic of her family's North Carolina bed-and-breakfast. The diary chronicles the life journeys of Molly Petree, an orphan at the end of the Civil War who grows up to be a cultured lady. Alternating with letters from Tuscany letters to her grad school advisor, the diary entries form a saga of life in the South when the world was changing.

Girl Talkin'

These stories are heavy on dialogue.

Hughley, Carolyn
Cupid's Web. 2007. Avalon. ISBN 0803498543. 266p.

Smart-aleck Cassie leaves small-town New Jersey for a marketing job in New York City. She's also happy to leave her ex-fiancé and her matchmaking mother behind. It's time to take control of her life, and get herself established in a career before settling down. She soon finds herself pursued by three different men, however, leading her to think perhaps having a real relationship can go hand in hand with living a real life. Snappy dialogue marks this entertaining light romantic tale.

Ireland, Perrin
Chatter. 2007. Algonquin Books of Chapel Hill. ISBN 9781565125407. 256p.

Michael and Sarah are a middle-aged couple whose lives are upended when the daughter Michael never knew he had appears on their doorstep. As Michael goes in search of the girl's mother, Sarah feels unsure of her next steps, and contemplates an affair. The novel is a chatty and fast paced, blur of communication (and miscommunication).

Kendrick, Beth
Fashionably Late. 2006. Downtown Press. ISBN 074349959X. 320p.

Becca moves to Los Angeles in order to escape her controlling ex-boyfriend, overprotective parents, and all-around boring life. After moving in with her sister, she pursues a career in fashion, and quickly begins to turn her life around. The fast and fun dialogue from the sisters is a standout in this title.

Landvik, Lorna
The Tall Pine Polka. 1999. Ballantine. ISBN 0345433173. 440p.

Told mostly in dialogue, this is the story of the regulars who spend their time at the Cup O'Delight Cafe in Tall Pine, Minnesota. There's owner Lee, who ran away from her abusive husband; lesbian couple Frau Katte and Miss Penk; and young Fenny Ness, who runs the local bait and tackle shop but is discovered by Hollywood agents who are scouting the area for a movie shoot. Wacky characters and a loving look at the friendships you can only find in an eccentric small town.

Meister, Ellen
Secret Confessions of the Applewood PTA. 2006. William Morrow. ISBN 0060818638. 320p.

Three different women become friends when they work together to get George Clooney to come to town. As directors of the publicity committee for their Applewood, Long Island, PTA, their job is to convince Hollywood producers, scouting a new movie site, that Applewood is the place to be. However, secretly, they are not so sure their hometown really holds that many charms, at least, not for themselves. Maddie has an inferiority complex that threatens her marriage, Ruth is having an affair to escape dealing with a sick husband, and Lisa is struggling to come to terms with her alcoholic mother, who wants to move in while she attends a nearby rehab center. Each woman has a fully developed, sharp, and sassy voice.

Smith, Lee
⇨ *The Last Girls.* 2002. ISBN 1565123638. 400p.

Twelve co-eds take a river rafting trip down in Mississippi in 1965. Nearly 35 years later, four of them gather together for another trip, this time on a luxury riverboat instead of a raft. The women tell each other what's happened in their lives since the last outing. Anna is a romance author; Courtney is a society maven; Catherine is happily married; and Harriet is a repressed schoolteacher. The scene shifts from past to present, with lots of dialogue in each woman's individual voice.

Literary Lasses

Sometimes, it can be difficult to differentiate general women's fiction from literary or mainstream fiction. These writers have a decidedly more serious, literate tone, where the language is elegant and the descriptions abound, but the heart of their novels are still the women's lives and relationships.

Davis, Amanda
Wonder When You'll Miss Me. 2003. William Morrow. ISBN 0688167810. 259p.

> Faith is haunted by the fat girl she used to be, who follows her around in her mind giving advice. She's also haunted by the memory of a brutal assault and her subsequent suicide attempt. Finally she decides to run away with the circus—literally. She joins the motley crew of the traveling Fartlesworth Circus, grooming the animals and befriending misfits as she tries to make her way through her mixed-up emotions. A powerfully written story, with strong characters.

Den Hartog, Kristen
Water Wings. 2003. MacAdam Cage. ISBN 1931561613. 269p.

> Considerable detail and artful phrasing mark this tale of family drama. Darlene is set to re-marry, and her family isn't quite sure how they feel about the decision. Her two grown daughters, their aunt, and their cousin all narrate chapters describing family secrets and the past.

Goodman, Carol
⇨ *The Sonnet Lover.* 2007. Ballantine. ISBN 9780345479570. 368p.

> Rose, a poet and Renaissance history teacher at a small college, gets a chance to go abroad to the school's Florentine villa to research a possible missing Shakespeare sonnet. Mysteries past and present abound, and Rose uncovers more than she bargained for while making decisions about her life and relationships. Goodman's novels are hard to pigeonhole—they contain elements of mystery, suspense, romance, and history—but strong women and their relationships are always at the core.

Prager, Emily
Eve's Tattoo. 1992. Vintage. ISBN 0679740538. 194p.

> Eve becomes obsessed with the photograph she sees of an Auschwitz prisoner, and on her 40th birthday, gets a tattoo of the woman's concentration camp number. She then begins a search for the woman's identity, which leads to startling results. A search for her own identity is the underlying theme of this literate and haunting novel.

Shreve, Anita
Body Surfing: A Novel. 2007. Little, Brown. ISBN 9780316059855. 304p.

> Sydney has had a hard romantic life. Only 29, she's endured divorce and widowhood. When she retreats to New Hampshire to tutor a teenage girl, Julie, she hopes it will be a non-eventful summer escape. Unfortunately, the family she works for draws her into their drama. Julie's anti-Semitic mother can't hide her dislike for half-Jewish Sydney; Julie's older brothers appear on the scene and both fall for Sydney; and Julie runs away with a secret. Dark drama and literary style are the highlights of this novel.

Sittenfeld, Curtis
Prep: A Novel. 2005. Random House. ISBN 1400062314. 416p.

Lee Fiora, a student at a prestigious New England prep school, struggles to fit in. A scholarship student from the Midwest, she doesn't have much in common with her classmates, nor does she care to be friends with most of them. When a popular young man takes an interest in her but wants to keep it a secret, she makes some very grown-up choices and deals with a broken heart.

Wolitzer, Meg
The Ten-Year Nap. 2008. Riverhead Books. ISBN 9781594489785. 320p.

A glimpse into the lives of different mothers who gave up their careers to have children. Now that their boys, all classmates at an exclusive New York private school are preteens, can they leap back into the working world—or do they even want to? Amy's feminist mother urges her to go back to being a lawyer; reserved and wealthy Karen goes on multiple interviews every month but can't see the need to work; artist Roberta fears she's lost her talent. A quiet, insightful meditation on women's work and what it means to be a mother.

Classics in the Field

From Austen to Woolf, here are the authors who started it all, writing about women's lives in their own times from the 1800s to the 1970s. (They are presented here in chronological order, rather than alphabetical by author.)

Austen, Jane
Emma. 1816. Reprint, 2003, Oxford University Press. ISBN 0192802372. 402p.

Rich, outspoken Emma has decided not to get married and instead, will play matchmaker for her friends, since she thinks she knows what's best for everyone. When she entangles herself in the romance of her friend Harriet, Emma realizes that perhaps she herself cannot stay detached from love. Emma is a delicious character who has been imitated in many a contemporary novel. Austen was gifted when it came to writing about women, and the small details of daily life in the early 1800s.

Brontë, Charlotte
Jane Eyre. 1847. Reprint, 1997, Modern Library. ISBN 0679602690. 682p.

Jane, an orphaned young woman, accepts employment as a governess at Thornfield Hall, a country estate owned by the mysterious Mr. Rochester. She eventually uncovers the secrets the house holds, and marries Rochester. The most intriguing characteristic of this novel is that Jane tells her own story, lending an intimacy to the tale, involving the reader at every turn.

Franklin, Miles

⇨ *My Brilliant Career.* 1901. Reprint, 2007, Penguin Classics. ISBN 0143105051. 288p.

Sybylla Melvyn lives in the Australian Outback during the 1890s, a time of political and social unrest. Sybylla is a young, spirited woman who rebels against convention of the times and the desire of her family that she be groomed to marry into a wealthy family. Instead, she heads off on her own, convinced that she will have a brilliant career. Franklin wrote this early feminist tale while she was in her late teens.

Woolf, Virginia

Night and Day. 1919. Reprint, 2003, Harvest Books. ISBN 0156028042. 516p.

Two friends living in Edwardian London try to determine if love is really necessary for happiness. Katharine is engaged to a stuffy man and longs to break out from her family's grip. Mary, on the other hand, is college educated, lives on her own, and works for the women's rights movement. Ironic humor and wit mark Woolf's tale crucial of women, marriage, and intellectual freedom.

McCarthy, Mary

The Group. 1963. Reprint, 1991, Harvest Books. ISBN 0156372088. 492p.

This novel follows a group of Vassar College friends from 1933 to 1940. The economic times allow these women to venture out for the first time, getting jobs and living on their own, reaching new social, professional, and personal heights. McCarthy, a brilliant social satirist, portrays eight young women on the cusp of something bigger than themselves.

Jong, Erica

Fear of Flying. 1973. Reprint, 2003, NAL Trade. ISBN 0451209435. 480p.

Isadora is a young poet, who, while on vacation with her husband, decides to indulge her sexual fantasies with another man. Shocking for its time, the novel's first person narrative is frank and the depiction of feminism in the 1970s is spot on.

Keep It Short and Sweet

Sometimes, all you have time for is a good short story. Whether you're at the gym, on the train to work, or catching a reading break at lunch, these short story collections are sure to give you your fix of women's fiction.

Anthologies

American Girls About Town. 2004. Downtown Press. ISBN 0743496957.

Seventeen stories from popular American women's fiction authors, including Jennifer Weiner, Lauren Weisberger, and Adriana Trigiani. In Trigiani's

"Chapter One: A Day in the Life of My Great Brit Book Tour," an author deals with traveling with her young daughter on a whirlwind publicity tour. Laura Wolf's "Amore" features a young woman on a quest to find an interesting foreign boyfriend, while Melissa Senate's "Voodoo Dolls, C-Cups, and Eminem" is a very funny look at a woman's need for revenge after her fiancé leaves her. Easy, breezy tales.

Girls Night In. Red Dress Ink. 2004. ISBN 0373250746. 352p.

Twenty-one stories from chick-lit authors such as Sarah Mlynowski, Isabel Wolff, and Lisa Jewell. In Mlynowski's "Know it All," the narrator's psychic roommate helps her out in the boyfriend department. Megan McCafferty's "From This Moment" is the tale of a wedding singer, while Wolff's "In Agony" features a mean-spirited advice columnist who gets a taste of her own medicine.

Girls Night Out. Red Dress Ink. 2006. ISBN 0373895798. 390p.

The follow-up to 2004's popular *Girls' Night In* features 25 more chick-lit authors, including Meg Cabot, Anna Maxted, and Cecelia Ahern. In Marian Keyes's "Wishing Carefully," Kate realizes that she should have been more specific when wishing for a fairy-tale romance. Emily Giffin's "A Thing of Beauty" finds Nina quitting her job and breaking up with her boyfriend on the advice of her manicurist. Fun and fast.

Crane, Elizabeth

When the Messenger is Hot. 2003. Little, Brown. ISBN 0316096520. 240p.

In her first collection, Crane presents stories of modern women and their relationships, mostly focusing on young urban women trying to figure out their place in the world. In "Something Shiny," a writer finds her life being taken over by the actress playing her in a movie. In "Privacy and Coffee," a woman decides to live on her friend's greenhouse patio in order to escape having to live her real life.

Dunmore, Helen

Ice Cream. 2000. Grove Press. ISBN 0802117333. 217p.

Seventeen stories from British author Dunmore, showcasing a talent for detail and character. In "You Stayed Awake with Me," two friends, one of them ill, revisit the past, while in "My Polish Teacher's Tie," a cafeteria worker longs for a life vastly different from her own. Atmospheric and somber, these may be very short stories, but they are not quick, light reads.

Miller, Rebecca

Personal Velocity. 2001. Grove Press. ISBN 080211699X. 179p.

Highlights of filmmaker Miller's first story collection include "Greta," where a cookbook editor finally becomes successful and wishes to leave her husband; "Louisa," the story of a struggling artist trying to make it in the big city; and "Julianne," the story of a woman who must come to terms with being the wife of a famous author. Lovely character sketches of seven very different women.

Weiner, Jennifer

⇨ *The Guy Not Taken: Stories.* 2007. Washington Square Press. ISBN 0743298055. 320p.

Weiner, known for her spot-on characters and often funny dialogue, gets slightly more serious in her collection of short stories. Several of them are autobiographical in nature, while the standout title story, "The Guy Not Taken," features a young woman who comes across her ex's online wedding registry, and tempts fate by updating the bride's information to her own name. Weiner also gives the reader notes on the stories, which gives some enjoyable background.

Index

117

About the Author

Photo by Ken Snyder.

REBECCA VNUK has worked as a Readers Advisory Librarian for several libraries and as a Collection Development Specialist for the Chicago Public Library. She is currently the Adult Services Director for the Glen Ellyn Public Library in Illinois. A fiction reviewer for *Library Journal,* she authored their Collection Development feature on Chick Lit in 2005. She has presented nationally on different readers advisory topics such as chick lit, readers advisory Web sites, and more. She is the 2007–2009 Chairperson of the Adult Reading Round Table, and was named 2008 Fiction Reviewer of the Year for *Library Journal.* She lives in the western suburbs of Chicago.